BUDDY

THE LAST CENTURION

Sam Harvey and Harv

WITH CHRIS McLEOD

Published by:
Wilkinson Publishing Pty Ltd
ACN 006 042 173
Level 6, 174 Collins St, Melbourne, Victoria, Australia 3000
Ph: +61 3 9654 5446
enquiries@wilkinsonpublishing.com.au

WilkinsonPublishing
wilkinsonpublishinghouse
WPBooks

A catalogue record of this book is available from the National Library of Australia.
ISBN: 9781922810892

Statistics sourced and based on data from AFL Tables, australianfootball.com, Big Footy, The VFA Project, AFL Record Season Guide 2021, WAFL Footy Facts, club web sites, newspaper reports.

Design: Michael Bannenberg.
Printed and bound in Australia by Ligare.

CONTENTS

INTRODUCTION

Would he retire? Would he play on with the Swans? Would he head north to a Queensland club for one last season?

These were the burning questions surrounding Australian Football League champion full-forward Lance (Buddy) Franklin throughout the 2022 season, his last under a nine-year contract about to end. What would 2023 have in store for perhaps the greatest goal-kicking forward of all time?

He'd found his way to the Sydney Swans by way of free-agency after eight seasons at Hawthorn. Injury and health issues had started to have an impact as he approached decision-time.

Sensing the end might be near, comparisons between Buddy and other greats of the game were inevitable. Was he the greatest player of all time (the GOAT)?

How did he compare to the other great goalkickers (five others had kicked 1,000 career goals and 27 others had kicked 100 in a season)?

There was much to discuss at the end of the 2022 Australian Football League season.

Buddy signed with the Swans on a reported $10 million deal in 2013 for nine seasons from 2014 (the most lucrative long-term deal in AFL history).

By 2021 speculation was mounting that his battle-weary body was about to give up, possibly sending the superstar full-forward into retirement after an AFL career that began when he was drafted by Hawthorn in 2004.

As well as injury woes, he'd missed seasons though mental health battles and Covid lockdowns. The future of the player regarded by many as the all-time greatest, was up in the air.

Pundits began talking about his greatest games, greatest goals and greatest marks.

His record speaks volumes for what he has brought to the game: he has kicked more than 50 goals in a season 12 times; won the Coleman Medal four times – 2008, 2011, 2014 and 2017; named in the All-Australian team eight times (captain in 2018); ranks equal fourth with Leigh Matthews for most goals in finals (72); one of eight First Nations players to play 300 AFL games.

As a key left-foot kicker up forward, Buddy proved to be a difficult match-up. His size (199 centimetres tall and weighing 106 kgs) combined with amazing athleticism made him a rare kind of footballer.

He changed the way the game was played, particularly as a mobile forward.

Goalkicking was his job. He had scored the goal of the year (and possibly the runner up as well) in one quarter playing against Essendon at the MCG in 2010.

He was still in form 11 years later on his return to the AFL after nearly 600 days (the last round in 2019) with a long bomb from outside 50 metres – after being told to play on by the umpire by way of a new rule about players standing the mark being able to move in once the kicker moved off line (Buddy's usual style was to run in an arc when kicking).

Commentator and former player Jonathon Brown commented: "But that was fantastic. He probably didn't need the run-up and play on anyway because he can kick it 60 metres!"

Shades of a younger Buddy!

He'd be turning 36 in January 2023, a few months before the start of the season, making him the oldest player on AFL lists, the last remaining player from the 2004 draft after Eddie Betts retired at the end of 2021.

His massive contract was due to end, but could he eke out another season?

In the week before the Grand Final against Geelong, Buddy announced his decision. He was playing on... with the Swans.

Many commentators had linked him to a move that would see him finish his career at Brisbane or even the Gold Coast where he and wife Jesinta had just bought a house after selling up in Sydney.

He had even considered ending his celebrated AFL career after the 2022 Grand Final, saying the decision to keep playing had been a "50-50" call.

In the end, he decided he still had the passion and would extend his career into an 18th season, his decision encouraged by wife Jesinta. The Franklin family was going to stick with Sydney in the AFL for most likely his last season, although he didn't specifically rule out anything.

The 2023 AFL fixture had Franklin (if fit and able) slated to play his last home-and-away game at the MCG against Richmond in Round 17, and his last home-and-away match in his home state, Western Australia, against Fremantle in Round 19.

Swans fans would have the chance to farewell Buddy at the SCG in his last home-and-away game in Round 24 against the Melbourne Demons. (If Sydney contested the finals, that scenario could be revised, of course).

The loss in the 2022 Grand Final on 24 September was a big disappointment for everyone connected with the Swans, Buddy and supporters alike.

It was the 127th Grand Final of the AFL, attended by 100,024 spectators. There was no way of dressing it up – the Swans capitulated big time, Geelong winning by 81 points for the Cats' tenth VFL/AFL premiership. The final score: Geelong 20.13 (133) defeated the Swans 8.4 (52).

Buddy failed to kick a goal and managed just a single behind. The four-time Coleman Medallist was shut out by Geelong youngster Jack Henry who kept him to just two marks, five kicks and five disposals. He managed only a ranking of 3 (of a possible 10) in the AFL player ratings for the match.

But there'd been a massive 2022 Buddy highlight before the finals when he became just the sixth player in the history of the VFL/AFL to kick career 1,000 goals.

Perhaps ironically his 1,000th goal came against Geelong, at a Swans home game at the SCG on 25 March 2022, in Round 2. His milestone goal, his fourth for the night, came late in the fourth quarter.

Buddy was mobbed by teammates and supporters as the Foo Fighters' classic *My Hero* played over the speakers at the ground. His 4 goals for the night helped the Swans to a 17.5 (107) to 10.17 (77) win over Geelong, a feat that unfortunately the Sydneysiders were unable to repeat in the "big dance" at the MCG six months later.

The scene at the Sydney Cricket Ground when he potted a six-pointer from a set shot 30 metres out will live long in the memory of fans and teammates.

Swans player Isaac Heany, an All-Australian player and at 26 years old and one of the Swans' leadership group later recalled the moment: "It was insane. It was one of the most special moments I've had on the footy field and it wasn't mine. I think the way he embraced it and the way he goes about things in my eyes he's the greatest player who has played the game. To share that with him on the footy field and him go away from that as well and he doesn't push his own cred ... he's so humble about how he goes about things and I love that about him and the footy club. How special that moment was, I feel privileged to have been part of it."

While the fans and Buddy will long remember that moment, the 2022 Grand Final loss stung.

Questions were asked whether the timing of his contract announcement detracted from the Swans' Grand Final preparation. Some journalists reported the Swans at first didn't want the announcement on a new deal, said to be worth $700,000, to be made until after the finals series.

As it turned out, the Swans decided that making the announcement that he was staying put before the Grand Final would allow the players, including Buddy, to focus on the game at hand.

The Swans put out a two-word statement: "One more." There was still a chance Buddy could get an elusive premiership with the Sydney Swans.

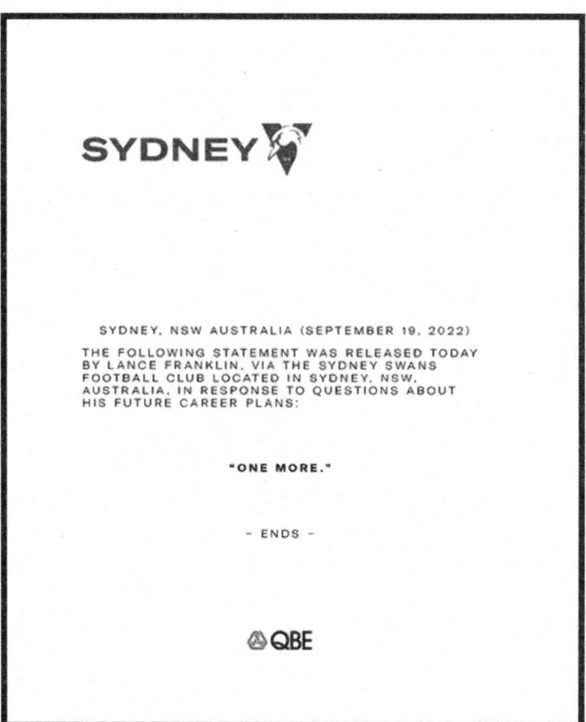

SYDNEY

SYDNEY, NSW AUSTRALIA (SEPTEMBER 19, 2022)

THE FOLLOWING STATEMENT WAS RELEASED TODAY BY LANCE FRANKLIN, VIA THE SYDNEY SWANS FOOTBALL CLUB LOCATED IN SYDNEY, NSW, AUSTRALIA, IN RESPONSE TO QUESTIONS ABOUT HIS FUTURE CAREER PLANS:

"ONE MORE."

- ENDS -

QBE

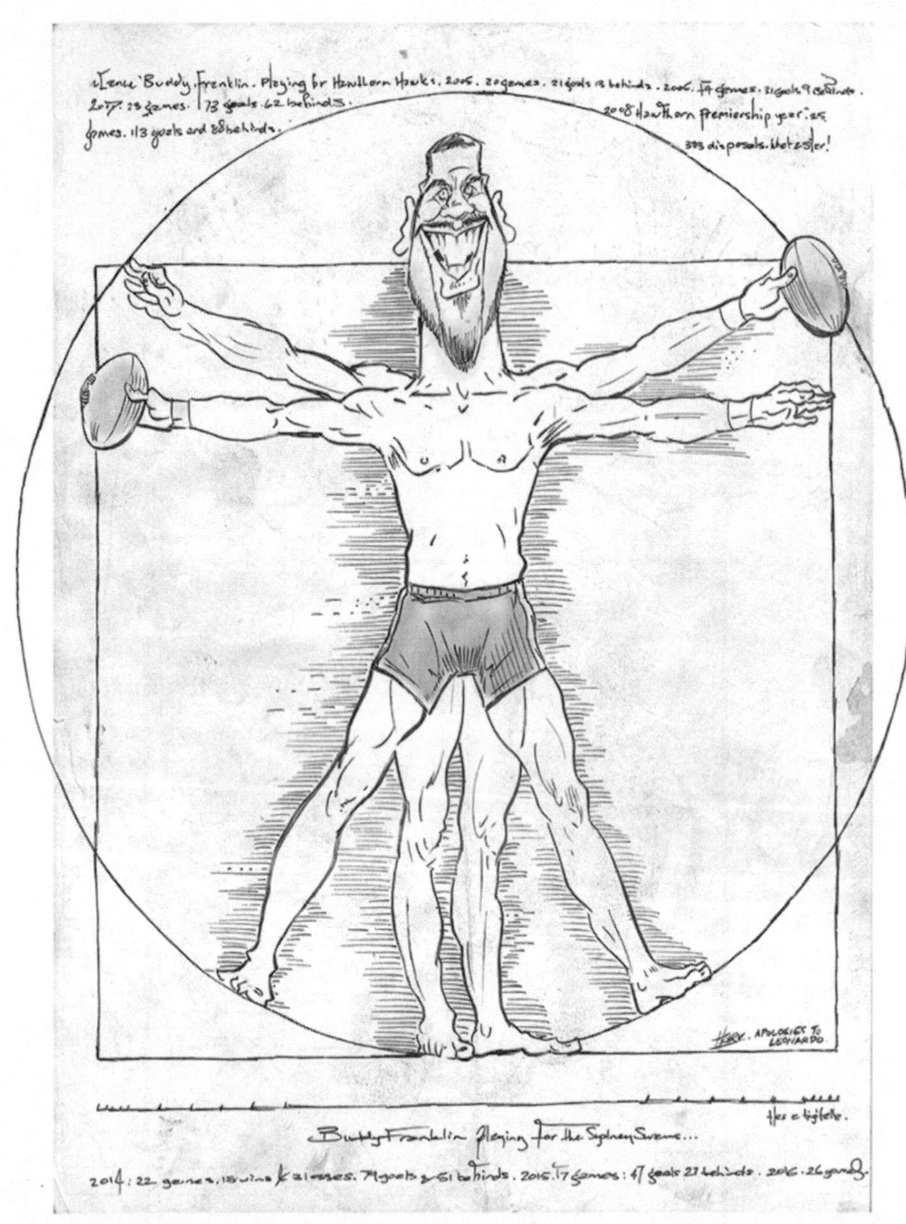

2007. 23 games. 73 goals. 62 behinds.
2008 Hawthorn premiership year: 25 games. 113 goals and 88 behinds.
APOLOGIES TO LEONARDO
Buddy Franklin playing for the Sydney Swans...

THE VITRUVIAN MAN

Regarded as one of the most iconic images in Western Civilization, the Vitruvian Man was a pen and ink drawing by the great Leonardo da Vinci around 1490. The artwork depicted the "ideal body proportion", and it is important because it was one of the first significant sketches depicting art and mathematics working in harmony.

During the Renaissance there were many philosophers who championed Humanism: to emphasize the social and individual potential of human beings. Vitruvian Man is at the centre of the universe. It is regarded as the epitome of human proportion, human perfection.

Lance Franklin is the Australian Rules "Vitruvian Man."

From the moment he ran a 40 second 300m at Dendy Park in Brighton, his first fitness session with Hawthorn, Buddy proved he was something special.

We all remember that famous running goal when Essendon defender Cale Hooker chased him haplessly from the wing. We can recall the 75m goal on a wet day at the MCG in front of 72,000 when he received a handball from Ben Stratton, hurdled Collingwood's number 41, Sam Dwyer, and hit a long range shot from well inside the square. We knew then this man was elite: we pondered whether the man was built in a test tube; or on Krypton.

Buddy is the perfect physical specimen for an AFL footballer. At 199cm tall, with a wingspan just over 2m, Franklin has the size and build to match some of the greatest sportsmen in history.

Buddy shares similar physical traits to NBA legend Michael Jordan, who is considered as the greatest basketball player ever, human-fish Michael Phelps, and the fastest man on earth Usain Bolt.

Not only is Franklin taller than these men, world sport's finest, but he has also worked tirelessly on his craft to become "The Vitruvian Man."

Franklin increased his 2007 draft size of 87kg to 105kg yet has lost none of his pace.

Usain Bolt from Jamaica is the most decorated Olympic sprinter in history, winning eight Olympic Gold medals at three different Games. Bolt defies sprinting physics with his 195cm frame, which is unusually tall for a sprinter. He is notorious for slowly starting his 100m and 200m sprints before overwhelming his opponents and powering home, using his natural long legs.

Buddy's speed has always been his greatest tool. It is Hawthorn footy folklore that in Franklin's first pre-season, he ran 20 x 150m sprints at 18 seconds apiece, beating everyone at the club. Usain Bolt's fastest official 150m was 14.35 seconds.

Undoubtedly the greatest athlete to ever jump in the pool, Michael Phelps is the most decorated Olympian in history, with 18 Gold Medals. With a wingspan of 201cm, a long torso to help him glide through the water and shorter legs that reduced his drag, Michael Phelps was built to swim. Like Franklin, Phelps is the prototype body shape for his chosen sport and has created a long-lasting legacy.

Franklin's long arms outreach most opponents except the tallest of ruckmen. Buddy then has the wheels to burn away from any ruck tasked with matching him in the air. His long torso makes him hard to tackle. He seems to weave through opposition arms.

As far as freakish athleticism goes, there's none greater than

Michael Jordan. Season after season Jordan used his competitive juices to fuel him to greatness. 'MJ' catapulted himself to greatness, and by the end of his career was the most marketable athlete of all time, with a net-worth of $US 1.7 billion.

On physical characteristics alone Franklin matches Jordan's legendary arm span and clears him for height. As a physical specimen Buddy is hard to beat.

The day Franklin announced himself as the next big superstar of the competition was on 8 September 2007, at the Telstra Dome.

The Hawks had finished 5th on the home-and-away ladder yet were licking their wounds after a 72-point drubbing at the hands of the Sydney Swans who finished 7th. This loss pushed Hawthorn out of the top four, and now they had to face the Adelaide Crows in an Elimination Final. The Crows who were 11th on the Ladder after Round 19, won their next three matches and defeated Collingwood at the same venue in the last round.

This was not going to be easy for the young Hawks side which featured 10 players aged 23 or under. To make matters worse, the Crows jumped out of the blocks early to lead by 19 points at quarter time. Adelaide had pushed out to a game high 31 points lead when their forward Ken McGregor kicked a goal in the 11th minute mark.

The Hawks were desperate for a hero. Enter Lance Franklin.

Three goals came off his boot in a five-minute burst and the Hawks only trailed by 2 goals at half-time. Hawthorn kicked a further 2 goals in the third quarter to bring the margin back to 2 points. The Crows rued missed chances, kicking 2 goals 5 behinds in the third quarter. When Buddy kicked his 6th goal in the 13th minute mark of the final term, the Hawks finally hit the lead for the first time.

The anxiousness of a finals victory seemed to have a deleterious effect on the young Hawks as they proceeded to kick 5 consecutive behinds to lose their lead. Closing in on the 29th minute mark and still down by three points, Hawks half-back flanker Ricky Ladson marked a short kick from stalwart Shane Crawford and sized up his options. It was a heart in your mouth moment when Ladson drilled a laser pass to Franklin, who would have the shot to win the game from just outside 50.

With what is now famously known as the "Buddy Arc," Franklin who'd kicked 2.11 two weeks previously on the same ground, calmly went back, and slotted the memorable sealer. He turned around to the crowd with his arms outstretched. He looked for all the world the model for Da Vinci's anatomical sketch.

From that moment on, Buddy's life changed forever, playing a further 181 games for Hawthorn, and 580 goals before joining the Sydney Swans.

The young Hawks, who had not won a final since 2001, went on famously to win the 2008 Premiership, with Franklin becoming the last player to kick 100 goals in a season.

If you took away Franklin's natural ability and athleticism, he wouldn't look out of place as a key position forward playing lower-level tough-as-nails suburban footy with his long kick and tattoos.

It is no lie that Buddy has struggled with marking the Sherrin over his head and has used his right foot fewer times than Australia has had Prime Ministers. Still, Franklin encompasses all the distinct traits that enabled the greatest forwards in the game's history to kick 1,000 career goals. Each of the great forwards has a unique quality that sets them apart. Franklin possesses the athleticism of Ablett Sr, the aura of Lockett, the unselfishness of Dunstall, the durability of Coventry, and the long, booming kick of Wade.

Buddy performed his miracles at much different period in football as well. A period, designed by myriad coaches to curb the influence of the forward as never before in the game.

In the 21st century it has never been full-forward v full-back, one out in the square, as it was in the 1970s, 80s and 90s. The tactical defensive mindset of many modern coaches has made defenders smarter; they intercept in the holes and zone off the space.

It hasn't been a picnic, yet Buddy has continued to be damaging. His trademark ability to break defensive zones and kick long-range goals from 50m+ continually has been able to counter even the most miserly team defence.

It may take footy lovers some time to digest the magnitude of 1,000 goals in the AFL era.

The Athleticism of Ablett Sr

Unlike the other predominant full forwards on this 1,000 goal list, Gary Ablett's athleticism saw him able to push up the ground and use his strength and pace to drive the Sherrin forward.

Lance Franklin shares these traits, and although they have kicked 1,000 career goals, these two aren't your typical stay-at-home full-forwards and only made a move closer to the goalmouth later in their careers. This is evident by the fact that Ablett Sr (12.85) and Franklin (10.70) averaged more kicks a game than Lockett (10.20) averaged disposals. Since stats were officially recorded in 1965, Ablett and Franklin are the only two footballers to average 15 disposals and 3 goals a game for their career.

What separates them from the other full-forwards is that even though they both liked to play up the ground, Ablett hit the scoreboard 1,721 times during his career at an average of 6.94, the same average Lockett had over his 281-game career.

Franklin has hit the scoreboard more than anyone in the modern century with 1,776 scores at 5.21. That is 569 more times than Jack Riewoldt, who has played 20 fewer games, and a higher average than Matthew Lloyd, who hit the scoreboard 1,350 times at an average of 5.00 across his 270-game career. Ablett and Franklin also share the uncanny ability to manoeuvre their body in tight traffic and find the goals. This is why they are regarded as the greatest footballers of their era.

The Aura of Lockett

There will never be another footballer who kicks goals like Tony Lockett. As far as goal-square full forwards go, Lockett is by far the best.

Not only was he a dead-eye sharpshooter, but he turned that goal-square into a boxing ring. The hot-tempered forward only had to stand in the square and let his aura do the rest. Defenders were on high alert 24/7, ever cautious of his presence. He monstered them all.

Franklin may not have the hot temper or brutal physicality of

footballers from yesteryear, but he has the same aura as Lockett. The fear of embarrassment consumes any defender when they line up on big Buddy, for they know if they relax for a single second, they'll end up on a highlights reel that'll be used on countless AFL promos and remain on social media for a decade.

The aura of Lockett and Franklin transcends the football field. Both became too big for the footy hub in Melbourne, and both sought time away from the Australian Rules microscope by moving to Sydney.

Franklin signed on to the Swans when he was 26 and Lockett signed on at the age of 28. Lockett has the record for most goals kicked at the SCG with 295 goals at 4.92 from 60 games; Franklin is in second place behind Lockett with 258 goals at 3.35 from 77 games.

In Australia, it is nigh on impossible for a Rugby Union or even Rugby League star to market themselves in South Australia. It is slightly less troublesome for Australian Rules star to market themselves in Sydney – a National Rugby League town. All the Australian states jealously protect their own 'footy-code.'

When Franklin moved into the rugby melting pot of Sydney at the end of 2013 on a $10 Million dollar deal, he even transcended the state border rivalry.

The Unselfishness of Dunstall

It's hard to understand how a footballer who kicked 1,254 goals could be regarded as unselfish, but Jason Dunstall could've easily finished with close to 1,500 goals if he wasn't so team-orientated.

Blessed to be playing in a team with unquestionable might,

Hawthorn was a scoring powerhouse between 1982 to 1991. They played 248 games, won 186 of them, including five premierships, and kicked a whopping 4,375 goals at an average of 17.64 a game.

The Hawks' sheer dominance was due to the VFL's push to secure the services of some of the best interstate footballers in Australia*.

Now, this is no blight on Dunstall's fantastic record; it just emphasises how unselfish he was in a dominant team. The selfless team approach is why the Hawks won so many flags during this timeframe. They had stars all over the park during this era.

Dunstall, between 1985 to 1991, only kicked 24.74% of Hawthorn's goals in the games he played yet still averaged 4.42 a game kicking 642 in total. Now, although Franklin was the focal point for the Hawks when he won his two flags at the club, he was also unselfishly team orientated like Dunstall.

Between 2008 to 2013, Franklin played 126 games, kicking 455 goals at 3.61, only kicking 23.86% of Hawthorn's total goals in those games. Looking at the Hawthorn side from 2008 to 2013, Franklin is fourth on the list for goal assists.

Hawthorn 2008-2013	Games	Goals	Goal Assists
C. Rioli	121	159	122
J. Lewis	130	86	101
S. Mitchell	136	40	100
L. Franklin	126	455	84
J. Roughead	126	1308	80

** The Hawks picked up John Platten, Tony Hall and later Darren Jarman from South Australia, Gary Buckenara, and Rod Lester-Smith from Western Australia. Carlton also secured four South Australian All-*

Australian footballers, Stephen Kernahan, Craig Bradley, Mark Naley and Peter Motley. By then, the VFL had no money to pay back these transfers, and by 1987 seven clubs were insolvent (Fitzroy, Geelong, Footscray, Collingwood, Melbourne, North Melbourne and Richmond).

The Durability of Coventry

Since the year 2000, there have been 35 players who have passed the 300 games mark, with 22 games per season, including finals.

Geelong's 2022 Premiership Captain, Joel Selwood, averaged 22.19 games a season for 16 years.

Let's rewind the clock more than 90 years when the Coulter Law* was in full swing. Players of all calibre were semi-professional and had full-time occupations on the side.

Collingwood spearhead Gordon Coventry was a boilermaker in

a yeast factory before becoming a foreman. His durability as a player, as well as a forward, is legendary.

In Round 11, 1935, "Nuts" broke Vic Thorp's games record of 263 before at last becoming the first V/AFL footballer to pass the 300-game mark, which he did in Round 15, 1937, against Footscray at the Western Oval. (Coventry, at the time, was 18 years older than his teammate Des Fothergill who finished the day with 5 goals at 17 years of age).

Franklin equalled Coventry's feat of 300 games and 1,000 goals in 2022 year and has shown his durability by kicking 50 or more goals in a season 13 times, drawing level with Coventry's effort.

When Coventry finished his decorated career, he was (and still is) the only player to kick 100 or more goals in finals, finishing with 111 at 3.58.

Like Coventry, Franklin has the most in the modern era and is third overall with 74 at 2.64, leading Alastair Lynch at 65, Peter Sumich at 62, Wayne Carey at 60, and Tom Hawkins at 56.

**Before the start of the 1930 season, players were paid £3 a game, with only captains or coaches paid more, with bonuses of up to £2 could be paid by the club. Most clubs at the time were allowed to offer employment through officials and supporters.*

The Long Booming Kick of Wade

When Lance Franklin kicked his first goal in the fourth minute mark of the first quarter against the West Coast Eagles in Round 1 2018, he broke the record for the most goals kicked playing in the jumper number 23.

After playing his first season in number 38, Franklin at the start of the 2023 season had kicked 1,049 goals. The player whose record was broken in 2018 was that of another 1,000 goal kicker, Geelong and North Melbourne's Doug Wade.

After Coventry kicked his 1,000th goal on the 4 June 1934, no player had cracked the 1,000 club until Doug Wade 40 years later when he kicked his second goal in North Melbourne's 38-point qualifying final win against Hawthorn in 1974.

As far as similarities go, Wade and Franklin are chalk and cheese. Buddy loves to get up the ground, Wade's home was the goal-square where he used his large frame to ride the backs of hapless defenders.

As is the norm now in the 21st century, players, especially forwards, use the drop punt when lining up for a set shot, Franklin is synonymous with his left leg that can find the goals with a drop punt from any angle. Wade on the other hand kicked towering torpedoes and flat punts.

Remarkably, Wade didn't kick a drop punt in a game, until he moved to North Melbourne in 1972, where the flat punt and drop kick was outlawed by legendary coach Ron Barassi. Although these two mighty forwards are opposites with their forward craft, they both won Coleman Medals at two different clubs and used their long booming kicking to devastating effect.

Most goals in #23	Games	Goals	Goal Average
L. Franklin	320	1021	3.19
D. Wade	208	834	4.01
S. Loewe	313	588	1.88
J.Peck	213	475	2.23
D. Brereton	187	422	2.26

NEVER SAY NEVER

SAM HARVEY

Great players have always been compartmentalised with questions such as, "Who is the greatest full-forward?", "Who is the greatest midfielder?", "Pick one, Lockett or Dunstall?" These questions have been debated myriad times over a few pots at the local watering hole.

Comparing past greats is tricky as each era of Australian Rules football has been played very differently. I decided to do a statistical breakdown of the illusive 100-goal mark and pinpoint why past greats have been able to achieve it.

I discovered some interesting variables. There has been a direct correlation between the introduction of certain rules and the increase in scoring.

Interestingly, there has also been a link between weather conditions, depending on whether Australia was in El Nino or La Nina. The dryer the season, the higher the scoring.

The increase in scores started in 1928, with the introduction of time-on in matches. A further increase followed the re-introduced the flick-pass*. The flick-pass allowed players to move the ball with greater speed, avoiding congestion.

The table below shows the gradual increase in scoring, coinciding with the rule changes.

1928	1929	1930	1931	1932	1933	1934	1935
79.46	77.23	80.56	76.42	81.94	86.02	92.28	89.38

1936	1937	1938	1939	1940	1941	1942
91.16	88.42	92.33	91.68	90.13	93.56	91.68

The weather has also played a significant role with scoring over the years. Since World War II, the average score has only dropped below 71 three times, in 1952, 1956 and 1960. Between 1954-57, Australia was experiencing its very own La Niña, with 1960 breaking the record for the wettest year on record down under. From the other spectrum, the 1980s were a high-scoring era, with the average reaching its peak in 1982 with 110.5. Again, there is no coincidence that this high-scoring year was due to Australia experiencing its most severe drought in the 20th century.

La Niña 1954-57

1954	1955	1956	1957
75.44	774.16	70.69	77.16

Eastern Australian Drought 1979-83

1979	1980	1981	1982	1983
104.5	103.3	97.7	110.5	104.1

** a player could use his open hand instead of his fist to propel the ball.*

During a chat with goalkicking legends Peter Hudson and Peter McKenna, they shared a unique insight on goalkicking and why players such as Lockett, Dunstall, Ablett and Franklin have stood out in their eras.

I've noticed, when speaking to these greats, that they're astute observers of the modern game, but they detest the word "compare". Initially I asked them which goal-kicking great is the "King of the Castle".

Hudson explained that the players had changed the game across the various eras, whereas most people believe that the game changes the players. I asked them both in separate interviews if the 100-goal mark would ever be achieved again, and both had different views.

Hudson suggested footy greats would kick goals in any era; they're regarded as exceptional forwards.

"People say the game changes the players, but I don't believe that. I believe that the players change the game... You put Lockett into any team in any era, and he will still kick 100 goals every time."

PETER HUDSON

Throughout the years, the role of the key forward has changed, just as the players have changed.

When Gordon Coventry kicked 17 against Fitzroy in Round 12 in 1930 the average height and weight for Collingwood was 177cm and 78kg. When Fred Fanning broke the league record with 18 goals in Round 19, 1947 against St. Kilda, Melbourne's ratio was 181cm and 81kg. When Franklin kicked 10 goals for Sydney against Carlton in Round 23, 2017, the Swan's dimensions were 188cm and 89kg.

The average height and weight of the 28 individual centurions is 187cm and 90kg. Lance Franklin is the tallest centurion at 199cm whilst George Moloney is the smallest at 174cm. Fraser Gehrig had the heaviest playing weight of 109kg, and Jack "Skinny" Titus is the lightest centurion at 66kg.

When Franklin kicked 73 goals in his 2007 break-out season, he was 3 goals off two-time Brownlow Medallist Peter Moore's 76-goal mark in 1977 for most goals at 198cm. The next year when Buddy kicked 113 goals he became the tallest centurion in history and the tallest footballer to kick 80 or more goals in a season, a feat he has achieved three times over his illustrious career.

Not only was Franklin a natural phenomenon with his height and thirst for goals, but he also changed the role of the modern-day forward in one single season, passing 100-goals during the home-

and-away rounds of 2008. No footballer had kicked 100 goals during the regular season since Tony Lockett, 10 years before.

With up to six coaches in the box working out tactics to stop the opposition from scoring, the role of the modern key forward has changed dramatically, and Franklin's efforts to not only kick 100 goals in a season, but 1,000 for his career, proves that he is a generational talent, with the likes of Lockett, Dunstall, Hudson and Ablett.

> *"For Dunstall, Lockett, Hudson and Wade, they still would be great players today because of their natural talent, but it would be harder to kick those monstrous tallies when all of those back men are crowding back on you... I often see Tommy Hawkins on the half-back line."*
>
> PETER McKENNA

Selfless would be one word to describe modern football. Players are more inclined to pass to a teammate in a better position, this has been drilled into them by coaches from junior football and this is the reason why a big bag of five or more goals is a rarity in 21st Century football.

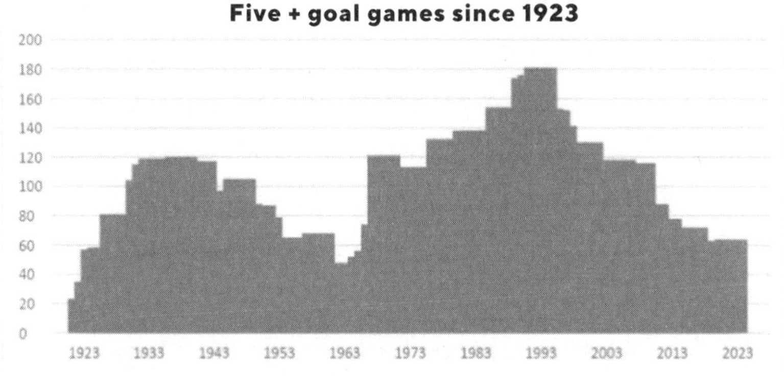

As you can see by the graph on the previous page, five-goal game tallies have fluctuated over the last 100 years. Excluding the 2020 season when quarters were shortened due to the Covid-19 Pandemic, 2021 with only 50 five-goal games was the lowest since 1965 which had 43. This pales into comparison when next to 1991 (174), 1992 (176) and 1993 (181).

"You don't see many big bags today, it would be much harder in the modern style of football, there's not the space to run into."

PETER MCKENNA

Across the past 20 years, Franklin has proven himself to be a one in a generation; he has been head and shoulders above everyone else in terms of five-goal games.

He has longevity on his side, having played more than 350 games, but by mid-2023 he had kicked more than Jeremy Cameron, Tom Lynch, Ben Brown, and Charlie Dixon combined, all key forwards at their clubs. Interesting to note, Brendan Fevola and Barry Hall are second and third respectively on the list. Fevola has been retired since 2010, and Hall has been retired since 2011, which shows

1. how selfless the modern key-forward is or
2. how good they are compared to Fev and big bustling Barry.

For a modern key-forward to kick 100 goals, they'll need two things: a side that makes the finals, and accuracy.

Only nine footballers in V/AFL history have passed the 100-mark without making finals. Peter Hudson remarkably did it in three consecutive seasons and Tony Lockett did it twice at different clubs. This feat would be nigh on impossible in modern football.

Outside of the top eight sides in 2022, Gold Coast kicked the most goals by a side that didn't make the finals with 271 goals. North

Five or more goals in the last 20 years (since 2004)

** Excluding the 2023 season.*

Total	Player	TM	Total	Player	TM
74	Lance Franklin	HW/SY	28	Eddie Betts	CA/AD
44	Brendan Fevola	CA/BL	27	Fraser Gehrig	SK
39	Barry Hall	SY/WB	26	Jeremy Cameron	GW/GE
36	Josh Kennedy	WC	26	Jarryd Roughead	HW
33	Jonathan Brown	BL	25	Daniel Bradshaw	BL/SY
31	Jack Riewoldt	RI	25	Nick Riewoldt	SK
30	Matthew Pavlich	FR	25	Tom Hawkins	GE

Melbourne only kicked 193 for the entire season. Even though Footscray finished second last in 1978 with a W-D-L record of 7-0-15, they still kicked 333 at an average of 103.7 points per game.

Lockett was the last to achieve the in-season feat in 1995 when the Swans finished 8-0-14 and kicked 343 goals. From the other spectrum, 14 forwards have passed the century mark in finals, with Matthew Lloyd the only one to achieve the feat twice.

Essendon's first goal-kicking icon John Coleman is the only forward to pass the century mark, with fewer than 90 goals going into the finals. (Coleman kicked 85 goals for the 1949 home-and-away season).

I guarantee if you walk into any footy-mad pub, there will be a dyed-in-the-wool old codger up at the bar saying that goal-kicking was better in their day. You can almost hear him bellow, "Hudson would've kicked that".

This is what we call primacy bias, the older generation tend to only remember the great big bags Lockett, Dunstall, Ablett, Hudson and McKenna kicked and have forgotten the shockers (Lockett kicked 3.7 in Round 2 1992, Ablett kicked 6.9 in Round 16 1995, Hudson kicked 7.9 in Round 22 1977, and McKenna kicked 1.10 in Round 10 1969).

We as footy lovers have at our fingertips every footy game on the weekend thanks to streaming services on our devices. Anyone, no matter how old, can watch and dissect every game with great ease, so of course they're going to see forwards miss the goals more regularly.

Over the 100 years of football, the least inaccurate seasons have been 1952 (44.93%), 1960 (45.18%), 1956 (45.19%), 1964 (45.22%) and 1953 (45.40%), whilst the most accurate seasons have all been in the modern era with 2000 (60.29%), 2008 (60.07%), 2005 (59.81%), 2001 (59.46%) and 2015 (59.41%).

Five or more goals in the last 20 years (since 2004)

** Excluding the 2023 season.*

Decade	Goals	Behinds	Accuracy
2000s	51180	35703	58.91
2010s	52198	36822	58.64
2020s	17955	13461	57.15
1990s	50552	37108	57.14
1980s	45183	36020	55.64
1970s	40644	34612	54.01
1930s	27501	29932	47.88
1940s	26809	29822	47.34
1960s	24019	26759	47.30
1950s	23317	27737	45.67

In the graph above you can see that the last three decades have seen the best accuracy in history, even with the introduction of more clubs and more goals kicked. Although with increased accuracy there have been only four centuries kicked since 2000 which is why it is no surprise that three of the top five most accurate 100-goal seasons were achieved 40 or more years ago.

Most Accurate 100-goal season

**Where stats are known*

Year	Player	Team	GM	GL	BH	Acc%
1970	Peter Hudson	HW	22	146	44	76.8
1998	Tony Lockett	SY	23	109	36	75.2
1969	Peter Hudson	HW	19	120	40	75.0
2001	Matthew Llyod	ES	21	105	36	74.5
1980	Michael Roach	RI	25	112	42	72.7

What stands out is Peter Hudson's unbelievable accuracy of 76.8% in 1970. This year doesn't get enough credit as it is still the most goals kicked in a home-and-away season as previously noted.

The Hawks only won 10 games, and Hudson kicked 44% of their goals. He kicked 146! If the Hawks had played finals and possibly made it to the big dance, Hudson would have obliterated the 150-goal mark.

Hudson's accuracy was as iconic as his famous flat-punt style that saw him go at 68.78% from his 727 career goals. Hudson still believes the 100-mark is attainable with accuracy: "People say no one will ever kick 150 goals in a season, well I don't believe that... the case I use all the time is Buddy, because he kicked 100 goals in a season and 80 behinds... with accuracy he's kicking more than 150 goals."

As a multiple centurion himself, Huddo's opinion on Franklin was very interesting, so I had a look at some of the biggest seasons since 2008. I measured their total score (Goals + Behinds), and I divided it by Hudson's goal-kicking accuracy of 76.8% in 1970. (See chart next page.)

With the accuracy of Hudson's 1970 season, we would have seen the 100-mark passed nine times since 2008, with Jonathan Brown and Josh Kennedy achieving the feat once, Brendan Fevola achieving the feat twice, and Franklin would have achieved the feat five times,

Goals with 76.8%	Player	Team	Year	Actual Goal	Goals + Behinds
154.4	Lance Franklin	HW	2008	113	201
122.9	Brendan Fevola	CA	2008	99	160
122.2	Brendan Fevola	CA	2009	89	146
109.9	Lance Franklin	HW	2011	82	143
105.3	Jonathan Brown	BL	2009	85	137
103.7	Josh Kennedy	WC	2015	80	135
103.7	Lance Franklin	SY	2016	81	135
102.2	Lance Franklin	HW	2012	69	133
102.2	Lance Franklin	SY	2017	73	133
99.9	Lance Franklin	SY	2014	79	130

kicking 154 in 2008, and finishing one short in 2014 with 99.

In more recent times, Jeremy Cameron would have kicked 96 in 2019, and Tom Hawkins would have kicked 84 in 2022. Maybe we as football fanatics should be more glass half full instead of glass half empty when believing the elusive 100-goal mark might never be achieved again.

With modern football strictly based on accuracy and efficiency, Lance Franklin is a footballing enigma. His powerful on-field kick has seen his teammates look to him for the answers to hit the scoreboard, often resulting in inaccuracy.

For the 2008 home and away season, Buddy kicked 103 goals and 84 behinds at 55.08% accuracy. More than 21.58% below Hudson in 1970. Franklin's 84 behinds equalled Jason Dunstall's 1992 home-and-away record (Pratt kicked 81 in the 1933 H/A season and Ablett Sr kicked 81 in 1995).

Franklin's penchant for spraying his shots on goal is emphasised by the fact he kicked 5 or more BEHINDS in a game 10 times. Brendan Fevola, who kicked 99 for the 2008 season kicked 5 or more GOALS in a game 11 times during the season. Buddy also kicked the ball through either set of posts 201 times for the season in 2008. The last player to pass the 200 mark was Gary Ablett Sr in 1995 with 207, and Bob Pratt has the record of 239, set in 1934.

200 or more scores in a V/AFL season

**Where stats are known*

Total	Player	Team	Year	GM	Av
239	Bob Pratt	SM	1934	21	11.38
229	Jason Dunstall	HW	1992	23	9.96
223	Peter McKenna	CW	1970	22	10.14
222	Peter Hudson	HW	1971	24	9.25
214	Jason Dunstall	HW	1989	24	8.92
201	Lance Franklin	HW	2008	25	8.04

Most Inaccurate 100-goal season

Year	Player	Team	GM	GL	BH	Acc%
1933	Bob Pratt	SM	18	109	92	54.2
1991	Peter Sumich	WC	25	111	89	55.5
2008	Lance Franklin	HW	25	113	88	56.2
1995	Gary Ablett	GE	22	122	85	58.9
1934	Gordon Coventry	CW	19	105	72	59.3

As far as 100-goal seasons go, Franklin's is the third most inaccurate of all time.

Bob Pratt tops the list with a goal-kicking accuracy of 54.2%. During the 1933 season, Pratt averaged a remarkable 5.11 behinds and 6.32 goals a game, that's nearly 12 shots on goal a game!

The last time a player kicked 50 or more in a season with under 50% accuracy was nearly 50 years ago when Essendon forward Allan Noonan kicked 77 goals and 81 behinds in 1974.

Since 1995, Franklin is the only player to kick 50 or more in a season at under 60% accuracy. Buddy has done this five times in a season.

The 100-goal mark remains an elusive target, yet it is interesting to note there was a large century drought between the years 1953-1967. When speaking with Sydney Swans official website in 2016, Franklin shared his own opinion on the 100-goal debate.

> *"I think it can be done, but who knows who it will be – there's a lot of guys kicking a lot of goals. To get 100 goals would be an unbelievable effort, but you've got to play consistently well over the course of the year. Play is opening up and there's one-on-ones happening, and as you can see this year, blokes have kicked bags of goals. I think that's what people love to come to the football to see."*
>
> LANCE FRANKLIN

PAST CENTURIES

SAM HARVEY

If my premise is that Lance Franklin is the greatest forward of all time, it is incumbent upon me to pay my dues to some of the greats from the past.

The 1930s heralded an explosion of goalkicking feats. It spread like wildfire through every football league in Australia. Even at the local level, goalkicking geniuses were being unearthed.

Not since Dave McNamara kicked 107 goals in the Victorian Football Association (VFA) in 1912 for the Dreadnaughts (a second Essendon football club known as Essendon Association or 'A' which played at Windy Hill) had a full-forward dominated any competition. McNamara is the first confirmed goal-kicking centurion in Australia. Still, the validity of the league is questionable, as McNamara once kicked 18 goals against Melbourne City in a game, from 38 attempts! This demolition would've looked like an 18-year-old playing against the under-12s.

Twelve years after McNamara's feat Jim Walsh, playing for Yarraville in the Victorian Junior Football League in 1924, kicked 133 goals. Although it states he played in the "Junior" Football League, Walsh was not a junior at the time, as the "junior" term refers to the fact that the league was the second XVIII to the VFA. Four years later, in the Ringwood District Football Association, George Bullen for Doncaster kicked 162 goals. RDFA changed its name to the Croydon Mail Football League before switching to the Eastern Suburbs Football League, then permanently to Eastern Districts Football League in 1962.

The feat had yet to be accomplished in any of the state leagues.

Anthony "Bos" Daly got close to the feat in 1893, kicking 88 goals for Norwood in the SANFL (Daly's impressive tally was helped by a 23-goal haul against Adelaide, which failed to field a full-strength team, and the game was played with 14 players on each side). In 1927, Collingwood's goal-kicking immortal Gordon Coventry got close, kicking 97. Some historians say Coventry would have achieved the milestone in the Grand Final of that year against Richmond had it not been for torrential rain that saw 3 goals kicked for the entire match (Coventry kicked 2, and the Magpies won 2.13-25 to 1.7-13). 1929 was the perfect storm. The powerful Collingwood outfit was dubbed The Machine due to its all-conquering run of four premierships in a row, achieving a 100%-win rate during the home and away season, all 18 games. If Collingwood was known as The Machine, then Coventry was the coal that fired its burners.

The rise of Coventry, 1926-34

The Magpies kicked 215 points more than second best, nearly doubling bottom placed North Melbourne which only registered 1,010 points for the season.

Coventry became the first state-league footballer to pass the magical milestone, kicking 124 out of the Magpies' 298 goals to become the King of the Spearheads.

The game had never seen anyone like him. Coventry was the quintessential Depression-era footballer, regarded by critics as more of a "warhorse" than a racehorse. He relied on his strong frame, superb judgement, and sticky hands to kick his goals.

Blessed with a fantastic midfield led by his captain and brother Syd, Collingwood's prescient game style of fast movement through the corridor, developed by coaching genius Jock McHale, saw

Coventry kick 938 goals at 4.99 between 1927-1936, winning six premierships and passing the century five times.

McHale's fast-movement game style was a direct result of the new rule, established in 1925, that saw free kicks awarded against any player whose errant kicks bounced over the line or were kicked out on the full.

Some of Collingwood's ball users, such as Harry Collier, Albert Collier, Jack Beveridge, Bruce Andrew, and Billy Libbis, were instructed to use the corridor as often as possible and knew that they only had to get it in the vicinity of Coventry, and he'd do the rest.

Unlike Buddy Franklin, who has blistering speed and the ability to do the unexpected, Coventry's repetitious style still saw him become the most prolific goalkicker in history, proving that full-forwards come in all shapes and sizes.

Most V/AFL goals after 25th birthday

Goals	Player	Team	GM	AV
1015	Gordon Coventry	CW	209	4.86
840	Gary Ablett Sr	GE	192	4.38
830	Tony Lockett	SK/SY	157	5.29
810	Jason Dunstall	HW	165	4.91
765	Doug Wade	GE	178	4.30
751	Jack Titus	RI	203	3.70
614	Bernie Quinlan	FO/FI	218	2.82
596	Lance Franklin	HW/SY	199	2.99
585	Harry Vallence	CA	144	4.06
575	Simon Beasley	FO	154	3.73

1930s Goalkicking Enlightenment

The 1930s was the golden era of goalkicking enlightenment. The life expectancy of goalkicking records around this period could be as short as just months. Some of the goalkicking exploits from local footballers and state league footballers around Australia will never be surpassed.

In Victoria, playing in the Metropolitan Amateur Football Association (now known as the VAFA), a man by the name of Alan La Fontaine created headlines kicking 168 goals for University Blacks, finishing the year with 197 thanks to another 29 goals in representative matches.

La Fontaine only scraped through by the skin of his teeth; remarkably, Old Scotch full-forward Bill Pearson finished the year on 163. La Fontaine would go on to have a decorated football career, captaining Melbourne to a hat-trick of premierships between 1939 and 1941, and winning four best-and-fairest awards, a record he holds with 1991 Brownlow Medallist Jim Stynes, and current-day champion Clayton Oliver.

Pearson never made it to the VFL, but boy did he leave an impression on the amateur competition. The next year he reached stratospheric levels becoming the first Australian Footballer to kick 200 goals in a season. Pearson's 220 goals included a 24-goal haul against University Blacks in Round 9, and a mammoth 30 goals haul against Brunswick in Round 15.

Pearson reached the century after 11 matches, and only needed another 8 games to reach the double century kicking a remarkable 83 goals from Round 14 to Round 18. Pearson's bags included 15, 30, 10, 11 and 17. He finished his career with 1022 goals from only 136 games at a remarkably high average of 7.51 a game. He kicked a 10-goal bag on average every three games!

Bob Pratt Pandemonium, 1933-35

By some mystical alignment of the cosmos, the 1930s saw each state league produce goalkicking superstars. The mercurial Bob Pratt from South Melbourne "Bloods", the nimble George Doig from East Fremantle, the reclusive Ken Farmer from North Adelaide, the utilitarian George Moloney who played in the VFL and WAFL, the perennial runner-up Ted Tyson from West Perth, and the spectacular Ron Todd who played for Collingwood and Williamstown.

Before Lockett and Franklin were kicking big bags for the mighty Bloods (Swans), a 21-year-old by the name of Bob Pratt created pandemonium in the VFL with his electrifying start to the 1934 season.

He started on fire, with 8 goals in Round 1 against Collingwood, followed up with a lazy 10 in a loss to Carlton, then blew the Bombers away with a 15-goal haul the very next week at

the Lake Oval (a club record that stood for 62 years).

He was kept relatively quiet in the first half, with only 3 goals to his name, and added another four goals in the third quarter. He then produced a masterclass, the most dominant 10-minutes of football in history, kicking 8 goals in the last quarter.

Young Pratt was chaired from the field at the end of the game and was given a round of applause from the supporters.

His purple patch didn't stop there as he cracked the quickest century in V/AFL history, taking only 13 games to reach the magical milestone.

Against Carlton again at the Lake Oval, the Blues raced out of the blocks early and held an 8-point lead at half-time. This lead quickly evaporated with the Bloods piling on 13 goals, 2 behinds for the quarter (at the time, this was the second highest scoring quarter by one side in history), Pratt kicking 8 goals to bring up the glorious 100.

He kicked another 23 goals in the next two weeks and had a remarkable 127 goals in 15 games at an average of 8.47 a game.

Pratt finished the home-and-away season with 138 goals from 18 games. The 150 mark was in sight.

In the first semi-final of the 1934 season, South Melbourne met Collingwood on the MCG, the new kid on the block up against the godfather of goal-men in Gordon Coventry.

The Bloods were eventual winners in an inaccurate affair, by three points. Both forwards were not immune to the pressure of this titanic battle.

Coventry's inaccuracy cost Collingwood, with the veteran kicking 5 goals 8 behinds. Pratt also had the yips in front of goal, kicking 4 goals, 7 behinds.

He bounced back the following week kicking 6 goals, 5 behinds against Geelong, and needed only two more to reach the impossible

150 milestone against Richmond in the Grand Final.

The Tigers and the Bloods were evenly matched; South Melbourne had the firepower up front and Richmond had a formidable backline. The last time the two sides clashed, South Melbourne lost by six points, in front of 40,000 at Punt Road Oval.

This time round, the Bloods were confident, boasting a side with Laurie Nash, Peter Reville, Herbie Matthews and Brighton Diggins.

Unfortunately, after a tight first quarter, the Tigers kicked 12.7 to 2.8 across the next two quarters before eventually winning by 39 points. If not for Laurie Nash, who had 25 kicks, 13 marks and kicked 6 goals 7 behinds, the result could've been even more disastrous.

Pratt failed to fire on the big day. kicking only 2 goals. Post-game, the tension within the South Melbourne outfit escalated with a punch-on occurring in the dressing rooms when some players were accused of playing dead.

It was well known that the "Catholic" South Melbourne Football Club showed little to no support for the Protestant players.

Achieving a feat never seen in any state league in Australia, wasn't enough for the powers-that-be at the Bloods. It is legend that Pratt was pipped in the Best and Fairest by Terry Brain, being told by officials, "Bob, you were spectacular, but you weren't very effective."

Pratt also kicked 89 behinds for the season. Pratt scored 989 points for South Melbourne off his own boot. To put that into context, Geelong's star forward Tom Hawkins scored 445 points for the Cats in their 2022 Premiership winning season. The most points scored in a season since the start of the 21st century was 766 by the star of this book, Lance "Buddy" Franklin in 2008. Pratt's 13-game century in 1934, is still the quickest in history.

The next year, South Melbourne finished the home-and-away

Quickest Century in V/AFL History

Player	Pratt	Ablett Sr	Hudson	Lockett	Coventry	Pratt	Coleman	Hudson	Wade	Hudson
TM	SM	GE	HW	SK	CW	SM	ES	HW	GE	HW
Year	1934	1993	1968	1991	1929	1933	1950	1969	1969	1970
1	8	7	10	12	6	5	4	6	4	8
2	10	8	8	10	6	7	11	4	4	4
3	15	14	8	12	11	5	5	6	9	8
4	6	4	5	4	2	6	8	4	4	3
5	7	12	5	7	6	5	5	16	9	6
6	4	7	4	5	8	3	5	6	7	8
7	6	3	3	8	4	9	8	0	7	3
8	5	7	5	5	3	5	5	6	7	13
9	8	10	10	8	8	7	6	4	7	6
10	7	5	8	5	7	6	7	13	4	5
11	9	11	6	2	7	10	10	2	2	7
12	8	5	5	5	7	11	4	4	7	3
13	11	5	12	1	16	6	6	5	6	3
14		10	7	13	4	5	3	9	4	9
15			6	10	4	5	8	9	8	8
16					7	7	7	6	11	11
Games	13	14	15	15	16	16	16	16	16	16

season on top of the ladder, Pratt pipping Coventry yet again for the leading goalkicker with 97 goals. Against the Magpies, Pratt kicked 10 goals playing on Hall of Fame fullback Jack Regan who was universally regarded as the "Prince of Fullbacks".

He passed the century mark yet again in the first semi-final against Collingwood, kicking 6 goals as South Melbourne ran away 21-point winners. The following week, Collingwood defeated reigning premiers Richmond, and would face off against South Melbourne in the Grand Final.

The Bloods were raging hot favourites with Pratt at full

forward… until all that changed when two days before the biggest game of the year, Pratt stepped from a tram on High St and into the path of a truck laden with five tonnes of bricks. He would not play in the Grand Final, and it was another 72 years and a move interstate before the Bloods won another flag.

Many conspiracy theories surrounded the accident, some suggested that wealthy Collingwood powerbroker John Wren paid to have Pratt nobbled. Pratt himself blamed legendary criminal identity Squizzy Taylor:

"I was getting off a tram when I was hit by a brick truck on the

evening before the 1935 Football Grand Final. I blamed Squizzy Taylor for running me down to 'fix' the match. I'd forgotten he'd been dead for 7 years!"

Bob Pratt finished his career at the Bloods with 681 goals from 158 games, a record he still holds at the South Melbourne/Sydney Football Club.

Pratt could have finished with even more career goals as he also missed his fair share.

Just as Buddy has struggled sometimes with goalkicking throughout his illustrious career, Pratt from 1932 to 1939 kicked 471 behinds at an average of 3.80, and kicked 613 goals at 4.93, passing the century mark on three consecutive seasons between 1933-35.

George Doig and Ted Tyson, Wizards of the West

Across the Nullarbor, the diminutive George Doig was creating headlines in the Western Australian Football League, playing for East Fremantle.

The Doig name is as big in WA as the Ablett name is in Victoria. In fact, 17 members from the famous sporting family played in the WAFL.

George's father Charles Sr played 216 games for East Fremantle, was named the leading goal-kicker of the competition twice and won eight premierships.

As a child, George played very little football at school, yet came into his own when he was playing for the East Fremantle B side in the Fremantle Suburban Association.

One day against Palmyra Football Club, Doig made newspaper headlines for the first time when he kicked his side's entire score of 26 goals 20 behinds. He finished the year with 126 goals.

It wasn't hard to get Doig over to the East Fremantle senior side, as his father was the president of the club.

The next year he played the entire 1932 season in the reserves kicking 128 goals, before making his senior debut the next year.

It was a memorable debut, kicking 9 goals against East Perth. He followed up with another 8 goals the next week on his way to 105 goals for the season. What a great way to kick start your career.

The season of 1934 was all about Pratt and Doig. Doig passed the century in Round 15, and after being kept to one goal against West Perth in Round 18, The Old Easts sharpshooter kicked 19 out of East Fremantle's 22 goals against Claremont in Round 19, and then backed it up with 13 the next week against Perth, finishing the home-and-away season with 144 goals.

Luckily for Doig, the WAFL played 20-game seasons compared to the VFL which only played 18.

In one of football's great coincidences Pratt and Doig both passed the 150-goal mark, becoming the first Australian State League footballers to kick 150 goals in a season, as fate would have it, on the same day, 13 October 1934. (Pratt sent Doig a telegram saying "congratulations on your great performance").

Doig's consistency was remarkable, he kicked 113 in 1935, 106 in 1936, 144 in 1937 (and 99 behinds), 100 in 1938, 105 in 1939, 107 in 1940, and 140 in 1941. Nine consecutive centuries is a legendary effort in any football competition.

If Ted Tyson had played in any other era, he would have been regarded as one of the greatest forwards in Western Australian football.

Tyson's lack of good fortune ranks him alongside The Netherlands National Football Team, which had lost three World Cup Finals (1974, 1978, 2010); the Buffalo Bills in the NFL, which lost four Super Bowls in a row between 1990-94; The Chicago Cubs in MLB with the 1945 "Billy Goat Curse" that saw Cubs take 107 years to win a World Series; North Sydney Bears in the NRL whose

Premiership drought lasted 77 years before they were banished from the NRL; or St. Kilda Football Club in the AFL, which has won only one premiership (1966) in nearly 150 years, losing four premiership matches since their dramatic one-point victory in 1966.

Tyson's story isn't as dramatic as those above, yet between 1934 to 1941, the West Perth spearhead passed the century mark six times yet only won the competition's leading goal-kicking medal once.

Tyson's main rival was George Doig, who won the award five times in those eight seasons. Although Doig is celebrated as the greatest Western Australian full-forward, Tyson remarkably had a better goal-per-game average between 1934-1941, astonishing considering Doig passed the century mark in each season. Doig kicked 967 goals at 5.56 from 174 games, whilst Tyson kicked 857 goals at 5.64 from 152 games.

Imagine averaging nearly 6 goals a game for a decade yet still being rated as the second-best forward in the competition. Tyson's finest moment came in Round 20, 1938, against Swan Districts. The final score was Swan District 18-15-123 to Ted Tyson 17-5-107. Yes, you read that correctly. Off his dangerous right foot, Ted Tyson lost to the Swans by 16 points, kicking 107 of West Perth's 115 points. Seventeen goals in a loss proves that you don't have to be dead to be stiff.

Tyson finished his illustrious career with 1196 goals from 228 games at 5.24 a game.

Ken Farmer. The greatest of them all?

Over in South Australia, whispers were flying around about a star full-forward who was even greater than Coventry, Pratt and Doig.

His name was Ken Farmer. This magician can lay claim to being the most consistent full-forward in history. Before Pratt and Doig kicked 150 each in 1934, Farmer had already kicked 613 goals from 105 games at an average of 5.83 for North Adelaide in the SANFL, including centuries in five consecutive seasons.

Before kids starting following John Coleman from end to end, kids from all over South Australia followed Farmer from end to end, season after season. Farmer's goal-kicking prowess saw him kick 1,146 goals at an average of 6.62 during the 1930s, passing the century mark in every year.

Vic Johnson who was a writer for *The Mail* and played on Farmer during his career for Port Adelaide, had nothing but adulation for the Roosters spearhead when he paid tribute to him after Farmer's retirement in 1941. Johnson said they spent countless hours preparing for Farmer and working out ways to defeat him. It was simple; stop Farmer and you stop North Adelaide. (Farmer kicked 42% of the Roosters' goals over his career).

That plan never worked, so they instead tried to stop every player in the North Adelaide side, nullifying Farmer's influence.

Farmer's finest moment came in 1940, when he kicked 23 goals six behinds in a game against West Torrens, breaking the record held by "Bos" Daly who achieved the feat in 1894. Retiring in 1941, he kicked 1419 goals in 224 games for North Adelaide at 6.33 and kicked 81 goals in 17 State games to finish with 1,500 goals.

Farmer became a recluse after his retirement, a self-described "worrier", he could barely stomach food before a game and spent countless restless hours trying to sleep. In an interview with Greg Hobbs for the *Sporting Globe* in 1980, Farmer delivered an interesting quote:

"Football used to worry the soul out of me. I took the game too seriously. I'd worry about a game in which I kicked a low tally rather than thinking of the good times when I'd kicked a bag."

This intense fear of everything was the result of a tragedy in which Farmer lost three family members in 12 months, including his brother Elliott who died in a motorcycle accident. Farmer was a pillion passenger.

"The Lord gave me the gift to play football, but he didn't give me the gift of handling it."

The goalkicking great's struggle with fame and the game is akin to Franklin who has had his fair share of trials and tribulations. There was no question that Farmer could have been as impressive in Victoria as he kicked 50 goals from 10 interstate matches against the Vics; averaging 5e goals a game against the best in the country is a remarkable feat.

George Moloney, the smallest V/AFL centurion

Although Farmer stayed in South Australia and Doig stayed in Western Australia, there have been a rare few who have dominated their state leagues as George Moloney did.

Known as "Specka", Moloney was before his time in the way that at only 174cm tall he could play in many positions.

Playing for Claremont-Cottesloe Moloney's breakout year came in 1930 when he kicked 78 goals playing at full-forward.

At the 1930 Adelaide Carnival, Moloney kicked 16 goals from five games for Western Australia, including a bag of six against Tasmania. After his dominant Carnival performance, Moloney was headhunted by the VFL, with Geelong eventually securing his services.

Much like a dangerous small forward in the 21st Century, Moloney was dynamic with his strength and agility. Once the ball hit the ground, he pounced like a hyena on a carcass and snapped brilliant goals. Seven goals on debut against the reigning premier Collingwood at Victoria Park was followed by 12 goals the next week against St. Kilda at Corio Oval.

Although he was quiet in the finals series, Moloney capped off his debut year with 78 goals and a premiership, kicking a goal in Geelong's 20-point win over Richmond.

The next year Moloney pushed his case as arguably the best player in the competition kicking 109 goals to be leading goalkicker as well as snaring Geelong's Club Campion award. He finished second in the Brownlow Medal to Fitzroy champion Haydn Bunton Sr.

Moloney had his fair share of shots on goal in 1932, kicking 21 goals 21 behinds across two weeks in Round 15 and Round 16. He kicked 71 out of Geelong's 104 points yet failed to even poll a single Brownlow vote. In the next game at Corio Oval (against Fitzroy) Moloney kicked 11 goals 10 behinds.

In his last year at Geelong, coach Percy Parratt moved his star forward into the centre of the ground. This was an audacious move at the time as many coaches, including Jock McHale, believed that players should not move from their positions, with all battles fought individually by the 18 on the field.

Moloney changed that idea when he won the Sandover Medal in the 1936 season for Claremont polling 30 votes and playing in the centre.

In 1939, the Claremont star switched back to full-forward with devastating effect, kicking 82 goals 49 behinds in 1939, 129 goals 52 behinds, and 108 goals 61 behinds in 1940.

By kicking a century of goals in 1939 Moloney became the first footballer in history to crack the ton in two different state leagues. Only two other footballers have achieved the feat since Moloney – Simon Beasley (119, Swan Districts 1981 and 105, Footscray 1985) and Malcolm Blight (103, North Melbourne 1982 and 126, Woodville 1985).

Remarkably, Moloney had a day out in Round 16 against Swan Districts in 1940, kicking 19 goals 9 behinds for the match to equal

Doig's record. Moloney went into the game with 80 goals and finished the day on 99, missing in the last five minutes to bring up his century.

Strangely, he was kept goalless the next week, kicking just 3 behinds, but finally passing the century-mark with 8 goals against East Perth a week later. Moloney finished his career with 858 goals (555 Claremont, 303 Geelong), which is a remarkable effort considering he spent five seasons in the midfield.

List of V/AFL footballers with 21 or more scores in a game

T	GL	BH	Player	TM	OP		Round	Year
24	15	9	Kelvin Templeton	FO	SK		13	1978
23	15	8	Gordon Coventry	CW	ES		11	1933
22	12	10	Norm Smith	ME	FO		17	1941
22	11	11	Fred Fanning	ME	HW		11	1944
22	17	5	Jason Dunstall	HW	RI		7	1992
21	10	11	Vin Gardiner	CA	SK		15	1911
21	16	5	Gordon Coventry	CW	HW		16	1929
21	17	4	Gordon Coventry	CW	FI		12	1930
21	10	11	George Moloney	GE	ME		15	1932
21	11	10	George Moloney	GE	FI		16	1932
21	14	7	Gary Ablett Sr	GE	ES		6	1993

VFA and the Throw Pass Era, 1938-41, 1945-47

With the 1925 "out of bounds" rule flowing over to the VFA (Victorian Football Association), head officials of the Association set about creating a schism within Australian Rules in Victoria by further amending their rules.

Looking to set itself apart from the VFL while trying to entice profiled stars from the rival competition, they legalised throwing of the Sherrin, naming it the "throw-pass".

Alongside the throw-pass, they also removed wingmen (16-men

sides), 15-metre penalties, no centre bounces, and boundary throw-ins.

Star players found the lucrative financial gain appealing; the VFL payment laws at the time, the Coulter Laws, only allowed players to be paid £4 ($5.67) a game.

In 1931, the VFA went to the ANFC (Australian National Football Council) and asked for the termination of their player-transfer contract with the VFL because they were now playing under different rules. By now being able to recruit the best footballers in Victoria without a clearance, the VFA became an exciting competition, with the new rules creating high scoring.

Harry "Soapy" Vallance who kicked 722 goals for Carlton moved to Williamstown, Ted Freyer who kicked 372 goals for Essendon moved to Port Melbourne, and the best footballer in the land, Laurie Nash moved to Camberwell.

In 1939, George Hawkins from Prahran kicked 164 goals (breaking George Doig's state league record of 152), Vallance kicked 133 for Williamstown, Lance Collins kicked 108 for Coburg, Harold Jones kicked 102 for Brunswick, and Laurie Nash kicked 100 for Camberwell.

With five individual players kicking 100 goals or more in a season, the VFA went one better in recruiting the best two forwards in Victoria, with Bob Pratt moving to Coburg and Collingwood spearhead Ron Todd moving to Williamstown.

Pratt's debut season for Coburg in 1940 was solid without being outstanding. He kicked 79 goals from 18 games, yet the following season, he brought in record crowds as he kicked a mountain of goals. In fact, Pratt obliterated Hawkins' record of 164 and set a new Australian state league record of 183 goals. In one three-game stretch, Pratt kicked 22 goals against Sandringham, 16 the following week against Oakleigh, and 11 against Camberwell the week after; 49 goals in three weeks!

Ron Todd, the new sensation, who shocked the VFL, 1938-46

Pratt wasn't the only hot property in the land of full-forwards.

After the past success of club legend Gordon Coventry, the Magpies found the next big thing.

Ron Todd was destined to be the greatest of the lot. He bled black and white. He'd been to every game since childhood and had the Magpies' first most outstanding forward, Dick Lee, as a family friend and mentor.

Todd made his debut in 1935 and spent his first two seasons in the same forward line as Coventry, the pair teaming up to kick 134 goals between them in 1937.

With Coventry near retirement, Todd knew his destiny lay at the goalmouth. When Coventry was famously suspended the week before the 1936 Grand Final, Todd was switched to full-forward and kicked 4 goals 9 behinds from 20 kicks.

Todd was taller than most forwards, skinny yet very agile, and especially quick over 20m. Todd's leap was legendary, and his hands were vice-like. Despite being a key forward, he found a lot of the football up the ground and would often finish games with more than 20 kicks.

1938 was Todd's season; he really set himself apart as one of the best forwards in the land, finishing with 120 goals.

Despite passing the century mark, Todd had constant goal-kicking woes and was said to have been too laid back in his kicking style, a statement often spoken about Lance Franklin.

In the Magpies' Round 3 clash against Richmond at Punt Road Oval, Todd had 26 kicks, 17 marks, 7 goals, 12 behinds and three out on the full.

The good outweighed the bad with Todd's goalkicking with an 11-goal bag in the preliminary final against Geelong. He kicked another 121 goals in 1939, including another 11-goal bag in a preliminary final, this time against St. Kilda.

Todd lived for the big moments, kicking 55 goals from 11 finals appearances and 28 goals in five games for Victoria.

In what would be one of the biggest "what ifs" in Australian football history, Todd dropped a bombshell at Victoria Park, declaring his intentions to move to Williamstown in the VFA.

Highest goals per game average in finals with 10 or more games

GL	GM	AV	Player	Teams
55	11	5.00	Ron Todd	CW
46	11	4.18	Peter McKenna	CW
64	16	4.00	Gary Ablett	HW/GE
53	14	3.79	Harry Vallence	CA
78	21	3.71	Jason Dunstall	HW
37	10	3.70	Bob Pratt	SM
65	18	3.61	Stephen Kernahan	CA
111	31	3.58	Gordon Coventry	CW
64	18	3.56	Doug Wade	GE/NM
60	17	3.53	Bill Brownless	GE
62	18	3.44	Jack Mueller	ME
62	19	3.26	Peter Sumich	WC
65	20	3.25	Alastair Lynch	FI/BB/BL
47	15	3.13	Dick Harris	RI
74	24	3.08	Jack Titus	RI
33	11	3.00	Des Fothergill	CW

After back-to-back centuries, Todd believed his contract was inadequate for his services. Williamstown's three-year offer saw the full-forward become the highest-paid player in any sport in Australia, earning £500 ($837.74 or $46,000 in 2023 terms) for the year and £5 ($8.38) per game.

To put that into perspective, Australian Golfer Cameron Smith, current Australian sporting-earner extraordinaire, earned more than $13 million in 2022.

In his first season for Williamstown as centre-half-forward, Todd kicked 99 goals for the season (Carlton great Harry "Soapy" Vallance kicked 113 at full-forward).

Injuries ruined Todd's 1941 season, and World War II was in full swing by then. While serving in the RAAF, Todd wrote to Collingwood expressing his desire to return to his original home Victoria Park and seeking a meeting with officials in 1945.

It was said that Todd was left waiting for hours as the officials bickered inside. Offended, Todd left Victoria Park humiliated, and Collingwood was left to eat humble pie as Todd reached extraordinary heights in 1945.

After 67 goals in his first six games, which included a 20-goal bag against Oakleigh, Todd passed the century mark in Round 10 and then passed the 150-goal mark after Round 18. By kicking a further s6 goals in the Seagulls' 37-point Grand Final win over Port Melbourne at the Junction Oval in front of 40,000 fans, Todd finished the season with 188 goals and the state-wide record firmly in his grasp.

Todd completed his footballing career with 1,001 league goals.

On the next page is a table featuring Pratt's 183-goal 1941 season, and Todd's 188-goal 1945 season.

3,437KM APART, THE TWO GOAL-KICKING MONOLITHS OF THE 1950S

Bernie Naylor and John Coleman were the goal-kicking monoliths of the 1950s. By the end of the 1951 season, Naylor had 587 goals in 129 games at an average of 4.55 a game.

At 189cm, Naylor was a large man for the 1950s and had a long

Pratt in 1941		Goals	Total
1	Brunswick	8	8
2	Yarraville	10	18
3	Williamstown	5	23
4	Northcote	13	36
5	Sandringham	12	48
6	Oakleigh	7	55
7	Prahran	7	62
8	Port Melbourne	5	67
10	Brighton	5	72
11	Preston	2	74
12	Brunswick	2	76
13	Yarraville	16	92
14	Williamstown	7	99
15	Northcote	3	102
16	Sandringham	22	124
17	Oakleigh	16	140
18	Camberwell	11	151
19	Brighton	5	156
20	Preston	9	165
1SF	Preston	8	173
PF	Prahran	6	179
GF	Port Melbourne	4	183

Todd in 1945		Goals	Total
1	Yarraville	9	9
2	Port Melbourne	8	17
3	Preston	13	30
4	Brighton	7	37
5	Oakleigh	20	57
6	Brunswick	10	67
7	Camberwell	6	73
8	Northcote	11	84
9	Coburg	10	94
10	Sandringham	11	105
11	Prahran	7	112
12	Yarraville	7	119
13	Port Melbourne	5	124
14	Preston	6	130
15	Brighton	5	135
16	Oakleigh	13	148
18	Camberwell	6	154
17	Brunswick	10	164
19	Northcote	9	173
20	Coburg	6	179
2SF	Coburg	3	182
GF	Port Melbourne	6	188

torpedo punt that he mastered due to the countless hours he spent practising after training at Fremantle Oval.

After kicking 61 goals in his first season in 1941, Naylor missed four consecutive years due to World War II. He returned in 1946 to kick 123 goals but hit his straps in 1952 when he kicked 147 goals and 80 behinds from only 21 games.

In Naylor's last three seasons of football in the WAFL, he kicked a remarkable 447 goals in 63 games, at an average of 7.09. His proficiency rivalled even that of Coleman, Farmer, and Pratt. He passed the five-goal mark 48 times and kicked ten or more 12 times.

In a nine-game stretch between Round 12 and Round 19 in 1952, Naylor kicked 84 goals and 44 behinds. Imagine averaging 9.33 goals and 4.88 behinds for three months!

Perhaps Naylor's finest hour came the very next season, in 1953. The South Fremantle spearhead started with 18 goals against

Subiaco in Round 2 and found himself with 79 goals by Round 10. George Doig's record of 152, set in 1934, was still the pinnacle of goalkicking across the Nullabor.

Heading into Round 14 with 95 to his name, Naylor would be facing Subiaco, the team he'd previously kicked 18 against. After a goalless second quarter, Naylor kicked 12 goals in the third quarter. Yes, you read that correctly;12 goals for the quarter. Naylor finished with 23 goals and 6 behinds and retired the following season after kicking 133 goals and kicking 7 goals in South Fremantle's 78-point Premiership victory over rivals East Fremantle in front of a crowd of 36,000 at Subiaco Oval.

After six flags since the end of World War II, South Fremantle was reportedly keen to develop some young forwards.

Naylor had an intense rivalry with West Perth spearhead Raymond Scott. They played against each other 30 times, with Naylor kicking 137 goals and Scott 132, even though South Fremantle won on 22 occasions.

The pair also played each other in 11 finals, kicking 41 goals each. Naylor finished his illustrious career with 1,034 goals in 194 games at 5.33. Scott finished his career with West Perth in 1959, kicking 910 goals at 4.62 from 197 games.

Even though the crowd was only 13,500, It seems like every Essendon fan and their dog was there that famous day when 20-year-old John Coleman kicked 12 goals on debut against Hawthorn. Still, it took this "overnight sensation" five seasons to become the talk of the league.

There was much hype around Coleman, after 296 goals in only 36 games for Hastings down on the Mornington Peninsula. Coleman had trained with the Bombers for two seasons yet struggled to make an impact in both preseasons.

You won't find a single footballer, who kicked 5 goals in their

first quarter of league football, yet Coleman was unlike other footballers. Training with Essendon in 1946, Coleman struggled at centre-half-forward and was banished to the back pocket. It wasn't all doom and gloom for him though; the club requested he sign a Form Four (contract) and play in the second XVIII.

After 136 goals in only 16 games in 1947 for Hastings in the Mornington Peninsula Football League, Coleman again trialled with Essendon, but his teammates didn't pass the ball to him.

By then 19 years old and aided by a growth spurt, Coleman kicked 160 goals in only 15 games for Hastings, kicking 17 goals against Seaford and 23 goals against Sorrento. On the eve of the 1949 season, 10 of the 12 VFL clubs approached Coleman, yet he stayed loyal to Essendon, which had lost the 1948 VFL Grand Final.

After 12 goals on debut, Coleman kicked his 100th goal in the Grand Final, gained selection for Victoria, finished third in the Brownlow, and won the Bombers' best and fairest. Can you name a better debut season?

Coleman, who at first struggled with the hordes of obsessed supporters following him from end to end, was undeterred on the football field, kicking 120 goals for the 1950 season as Essendon kicked 62 more goals than any other side, losing one game for the season and defeating North Melbourne by 38 points in the Grand Final. Clubs around the VFL tried to curb Coleman's influence.

Some full-backs played right up to his backside, others tried to match him in the air. All tried and failed.

Often facing up to three opponents every week, none could match Coleman's pace off the lead.

Like Franklin, this Essendon great galloped like a gazelle running across the African Savana. If Coleman was still alive today, he would fall off his rocking chair looking at all the tiggy-touchwood free kicks forwards get in the 21st century.

Countless times he faced hair pulling, physical abuse and even headlocks off the ball. This mistreatment reached its zenith when the Bombers played their arch-rivals Carlton in the penultimate round of the home-and-away season at Princes Park.

Throughout the game, Carlton tall defender Harry Caspar hit Coleman twice while the ball was at the other end of the ground. Coleman retaliated and was reported by the on-field umpire. Tempers boiled over in the players' race when a fan spat on Coleman's face. The star forward badly hurt his hand smashing the fan in the face.

Coleman finished the game with 7 goals yet was suspended for four games, costing Essendon the 1951 Premiership. It is said Bombers fans still curse the name Harry Caspar to this day.

Although Essendon moved down the pecking order, Coleman was still at his dominant best, kicking 103 goals in 1952 (44 more than next best) and 97 in 1953 (32 more than next best), and 1954 looked like it was going to be his most fabulous season yet.

After kicking a career-best 14 goals against Fitzroy, the superstar had 37 goals in only five games and was already on his way to another century before he landed awkwardly and dislocated his right knee the following week against North Melbourne. He never played again.

The way Coleman played changed Australian Rules.

The out-of-bounds free-kick rule exaggerated the success of the 1930s greats such as Coventry, Pratt, Mohr and Todd.

Coleman's success in the forward line came after the boundary throw-in was re-introduced, and the average score throughout those six years was 75.5 per game.

Compared to his contemporaries, between 1949 to 1954, Coleman stands head and shoulders above them all.

From the top 10 goal-kickers between 1949-1954, they averaged 25.4% of their teams' total of goals whilst Coleman averaged

44.17% of Essendon's goals across his career.

To further explain Coleman's dominance compared to his rivals, in 1950 he kicked 120 goals. Hawthorn as a football club in 1950 kicked 136.

1949-1954	TM	GM	GL	AV
Coleman	ES	98	537	5.48
Hart	FI	47	168	3.57
Goninon	ES/GE	85	282	3.32
Spencer	NM	93	304	3.27
O'Rourke	RI	44	134	3.04
Bennett	SK	73	189	2.59
Howell	CA	67	151	2.25

SENSATIONAL 70s

Hair was shaggy, moustaches abounded, platform shoes were groovy, Sunny boys were a favourite refresher, and seatbelts weren't mandatory.

1970 was also the year that full-forwards ruled the roost.

Carlton great Alex Jesaulenko kicked 115, Peter McKenna, with his Beatles mop, kicked 143, and Tasmanian superstar Peter Hudson kicked 146, the most goals ever kicked in a home-and-away season.

This was the first time three forwards kicked 100 or more in a season. The previous year was close, with McKenna finishing with 98, Hudson 120, and Geelong forward Doug Wade the best with 127.

Alex Jesaulenko

Jesaulenko's brilliant 1970 season gets under-appreciated compared to the goalkicking brilliance of Hudson, Wade and McKenna.

Jesaulenko's prodigious talent made him a far more damaging player in other positions around the ground.

I find myself wondering how many goals he would have kicked for the Navy Blues if he stayed at full-forward.

Regarded as the prototype modern-day footballer, Austrian-born Jesualenko emigrated to Australia with his family when he was three years old, settling in Canberra.

Universally known as "Jezza", he grew up playing soccer and rugby and surprisingly did not kick an Australian rules football until he was 14.

A trailblazer for many modern dual-sports stars such as Scott Pendlebury and Erin Phillips (Basketball), Jezza credits soccer

for helping him with his balance and rugby for helping with his toughness.

Able to kick a drop-kick with a rugby ball, Jezza developed a damaging drop-punt when playing for Eastlake in the ACT competition and shocked the VFL world when he used it regularly around the field and in front of the goals.

Like Gary Ablett Sr, Jesaulenko could break a game open in the space of 10 minutes and was prone to having shots from all around the ground. (In Round 2 1969, Jesaulenko was at his damaging yet inaccurate best, kicking 6.12 against Hawthorn as Carlton piled on 30.30-210, a then VFL record).

Jesaulenko was regarded as the most damaging player in the competition in 1970, kicking 40 goals in the first six rounds of the season. Five times, newspaper experts awarded him best-on-ground honours.

When Jezza kicked 9.5 against St. Kilda, playing on two of the best defenders in the game (Bob Murray and Barry Lawrence), pundits said the Carlton star could win the Brownlow Medal.

Facing Melbourne in the last round of the home-and-away season, all eyes were on Jezza to become the first Carlton footballer to kick 100 goals in a season.

With his Carlton teammates looking for him at every opportunity, the Navy Blues star was triple-teamed and kicked erratically in front of the big sticks (he kicked 5.6).

With a few minutes left in the final quarter, Carlton rover Adrian Gallagher deliberately passed the ball backwards to Jesaulenko, who kicked truly to become Carlton's first centurion. Always one to rise on the big stage, the next week Jezza kicked 8.0 in Carlton's 10-point semi-final loss to Collingwood, and then famously took the "mark of the century" over Magpie Graeme "Jerker" Jenkin in the Blues comeback Grand Final win.

Jesaulenko went on to have a decorated V/AFL career, kicking 444 goals from 279 games, winning four Premierships, including one as captain-coach in 1979.

Between 1967 and 1974, Hudson, Wade and McKenna took out the leading goal-kicking awards. Hudson and Wade both won three awards, whilst McKenna won two.

Player	TM	GM	GL	AV	Accuracy	7+ goals	10+ goals
Hudson	HW	105	617	5.88	68.78	26	11
McKenna	CW	152	771	5.07	65.28	32	12
Wade	GE	163	721	4.42	63.19	28	4

Hudson broke the 17-year century-drought by kicking 125 in 1968 (the most goals in a season since Bob Pratt kicked 150 in 1934). Wade went one better the following year with 127 goals before Hudson (146) and McKenna (143) kicked more than 140 in a season in 1970.

In six seasons, the full-forward role had changed considerably since John Peck won the Coleman Medal in 1965 with 56 goals.

Hudson v. McKenna, during the 1970s, was like two heavyweight champions battling it out.

Every young kid would hover around the radio to see who had kicked more and frantically check the papers to see if the leaderboard had changed.

In the nine clashes that the two went head-to-head, Hudson kicked 53 goals, 18 behinds and the Collingwood spearhead kicked 40 goals, 35 behinds.

From 1968 to 1971, Hudson kicked 541 goals at 6.44, passing the century mark four years in a row. McKenna, on the other hand, kicked 505 goals at 6.08 between 1969 to 1972, passing the century mark three years in a row.

Two forwards, simultaneously, averaging more than 6 goals a game across a four-year period is remarkable.

Even more amazingly, Hudson, McKenna and Wade kicked their goals with different kicking styles to significant effect. Hudson kicked the flat punt, McKenna kicked the drop punt, and Wade kicked the torpedo punt.

Watching videos of old games from the turn of the century until the 1960s, I can't help but notice how deplorable the skills are. The ball would bounce from one end to the other like a ping pong ball, with handball rarely used. Most footballers would hurriedly throw the Sherrin on their boot and launch it out of dangerous territory with a flat punt or torpedo. A flat punt is similar to a torpedo; the difference is that it does not spin like a torpedo. Forwards during the 1960s and 70s would use torpedo punts (where the ball would spin clockwise along its length), screw punts (similar to a torpedo punt, less aesthetic), drop kicks (where the ball would bounce off the ground before the boot made contact) and drop punts when kicking for goal, but it was "Huddo" that made the flat punt famous.

PETER HUDSON AND THE FLAT PUNT

Hudson's set shot routine was described as "a dog trying to make love to a tennis ball." It didn't look pretty, but boy it was effective as he finished his decorated career with 2191 goals at 5.89 from 372 games in Victoria and Tasmania.

He didn't soar above packs like Tony Modra; he didn't have the athleticism of Ablett and Franklin, but he had a great footy brain.

No defender in the country could put Hudson off his task because he had unwavering focus. When I sat down one morning in Blairgowrie for a chat with him, he explained how he would track the ball from one end to the other throughout the game.

Hudson knew that he didn't have to be the greatest leaping mark on the lead and go for balls in the air (risking injury) if he watched the ball's flight and memorised the kicking style of each of his teammates; these two skills he regarded as his major weapons.

> *"I would even follow the ball into the crowd and could tell you the colour of the coat on the lady it hit."*

When I queried the goalkicking immortal about the kicking style of some of his old teammates, his eyes lit up when he

remembered premiership comrades such as Des Meagher, Bob Keddie and Peter Crimmins.

"Des either kicked a nine iron or a two iron... he was such a long kick, if he got onto it, you might as well lead towards the swimming pool on Glenferrie Road."

"I knew exactly with Bob Keddie where the ball was going to go. Peter Crimmins, just led flat out, straight at him, because you knew he'd hit you lace out. To me that's the most important part. Knowing your team-mates. You can't kick a goal if you don't have the ball."

"A lot of people said I was lucky or the ball would just fall into my hands but I used to concentrate on the ball and I knew my team-mates. I knew where the ball was going."

"WHAT WOULD YOU DO IF JESUS CHRIST CAME TO HAWTHORN TODAY?"
"MOVE PETER HUDSON TO CENTRE HALF FORWARD."

Hudson remembered being constantly bombarded by this, possibly, apocryphal story of the graffiti in front of a church in Hawthorn. He said he once declared he'd be dirty on being moved as he had not once seen Jesus at a training session.

Not since John Coleman had we seen a forward with such a hunger for goals. Hudson's concentration was next level, he loved the defenders who would niggle him as he would know where they were and could use his strong frame to outmanoeuvre him.

Defenders such as Saints Premiership hero Bob Murray scared him the most as he played off him and jumped from behind.

"In the 1960s, the kicking wasn't as good as it is now, you had a lot of miss kicks... you had a lot of blokes that regularly miss kicked. If I knew how the bloke miss kicked and I knew where the ball was going to land, I'd go there. The full-back wouldn't have known that."

In his first season for Upper Derwent Football Club in the SDFA in 1962 at 16 years old, Hudson kicked 124 goals in 20 games, with a Grand Final victory over Maydena Football Club.

At the post-game celebrations at the Rosegarland Hotel, victorious Captain-Coach Bob Hudson (Peter's father) had a couple of beers with his teammates inside, while Peter, too young to be allowed into the pub, had to sit in the car with his mother.

After 378 goals from 75 games for New Norfolk Football Club, Hudson was the most sought-after footballer in Tasmania, eventually signing on with the Hawks.

After a slow start to his VFL career at Glenferrie Oval, Hawks coach John Kennedy Sr instructed his half-forwards to push up the ground and leave Hudson one out with his defender, 100m off the ball. Unlike the zoning of modern football, which has seen the importance of intercept defenders, Kennedy would start half-forwards (Bob Keddie, Geoff Angus) near the centre circle and instructed his midfielders (Leigh Matthews and Peter Crimmins) to get the ball down to Hudson as quickly as possible.

This tactic meant the opposition ruck couldn't jump in the hole and help his fullback because Hawthorn's centre-half forward would be near the centre.

Often Hudson would outwit his opponent, and the goals piled on.

Hudson's record between 1968 to 1971

Year	GM	GL	BH	AV	7+ goals	10+ goals
1968	19	125	62	6.58	5	3
1969	19	120	40	6.32	3	2
1970	22	146	44	6.64	8	3
1971	24	150	72	6.25	7	3
Total	84	541	218	6.44	23	11

Kennedy's successful "Hudson Plan" caused headaches for the VFL's administrators, who were frustrated with the congestion around the ball.

Akin to the 6-6-6 rule we have now in modern football, the VFL decided to introduce the centre diamond in 1973 (the VFL then changed the centre diamond to the modern centre square in 1975), which made sure that only four players (ruck, rover, ruck-rover, centre) were permitted inside for the centre-bounce.

After 102 games and 606 goals, including 8 up until half-time against Melbourne in 1972, Hudson landed awkwardly and damaged his knee badly.

Some still question what could've been if Hudson didn't get the injury. However, he proved that he still had the same ability when he arrived via Helicopter at Waverley Park in Round 21, 1973 and kicked 8 goals (still with his damaged knee) against Collingwood in a vital game for the Hawks.

Hudson's movie-star arrival was organised because he was busy running his pub in Hobart (he worked the Friday night) and had Norman Gunston (Garry McDonald's satirical TV character) appearing that night in front of a packed house.

Hudson eventually returned for one more season in 1977 and

kicked 110 goals from 24 games, proving he could kick the magical 100 even after such a long layoff.

He moved back to Tasmania permanently in 1978 after a decorated career of 727 V/AFL goals at 5.64 from 129 at Hawthorn and would kick a further 616 goals from 81 games at 7.60 for Glenorchy in the TANFL.

His last two seasons of state league football were outstanding for Glenorchy.

In 1978 he kicked 153 goals from 20 games, adding 21 goals in interstate games and 17 in intrastate games to finish the year with 191 goals.

On the eve of the 1979 season, Hudson announced he would be retiring at the completion. In what can only be described as the greatest swansong, Hudson kicked 179 from 21 games during the season, 16 goals in interstate matches, and 14 goals in intrastate games, passing the insurmountable mark of 200 goals in the TANFL Grand Final against Clarence in front of a Tasmanian record crowd of 24,968.

This achievement even saw him included in the Guinness Book of Records.

Peter McKenna

Like a young magpie discovering it can fly, Peter McKenna's footballing journey changed in Round 11, 1968.

McKenna showed glimpses of his untapped potential with 12 goals against Hawthorn in the opening round of the 1966 season, but after three seasons, he was being played out of position at centre-half-forward and sometimes at centre-half-back in the reserves.

McKenna would go on to kick 6.3 against South Melbourne after former Collingwood premiership captain and then media commentator Lou Richards described him as "hopeless".

At only 21 years old-old, McKenna was at the crossroads of his career going into that game. For the remaining 12 games of the 1968 season, he kicked 60 goals, including 11 against South Melbourne in the season's final round.

Collingwood had unearthed yet another star key-forward.

Between 1970 and 1972, McKenna kicked more than 130 goals in three seasons (143, 134, 130). Even at a club with goalkicking legends such as Coventry and Todd, McKenna's three centuries are still the three most goals in a season by a Collingwood footballer. A humble footballing great, McKenna puts it down to being in a good side.

"You need to be in a good side, and you need to have a good midfield to kick 100 goals… I was lucky to be at Collingwood at the same time as the Barry Price and the Richardson brothers with their kicking ability… Everywhere he (Price) goes, I get a mention, and everywhere I go he (Price) gets a mention."

McKenna had an aesthetic modern drop punt set-shot that rarely let him down. His liking for the drop punt was unusual as many forwards still used the torpedo punt, as many coaches saw it as more effective.

From the age of 8 to 13, McKenna played competitive soccer which he believes helped him control his timing and power.

Legendary goal-kicker Ken Farmer, who kicked 1,419 goals in the SANFL, and 81 for South Australia, had played soccer during his adolescence and was selected in the state schoolboys' side. Carlton Premiership Captain-Coach Alex Jesaulenko and the flamboyant Tony Modra all played soccer growing up, which contributed to their accuracy and power.

"I grew up in West Heidelberg near a soccer ground we used to have a little competition with each other, to try and kick goals under the soccer bar with the Sherrin and Soccer Ball. So we learned to kick drop punts, and kick them low and hard".

Fittingly, the side (South Melbourne) that rejuvenated his career in Round 11 in 1968 became a happy hunting ground for McKenna. He kicked 126 goals at an average of seven a game from his 18 clashes against the Bloods during his career.

McKenna remembers one happy day when he kicked 16.4 (100) in Collingwood's 19.15 (129) score at Victoria Park before 19,000 fans. The Magpies won the game by 71 points, yet the final margin should've been less, as a wayward South Melbourne kicked 16.22 (58).

Playing on Ron Wetzel, McKenna outmanoeuvred the raw defender (playing his first season of VFL football) and kicked 4 goals in the first quarter.

South Melbourne had the momentum in the second quarter but couldn't impact the scoreboard kicking 1.9.

Collingwood's new superstar forward broke loose in the third quarter, kicking 5 straight as the Magpies piled on another 6 goals to have a 37-point lead at three-quarter time.

After 3 quick goals to start the last quarter, McKenna had 14.0 for the match, and the eager crowd began to believe their star forward was on his way to passing Fred Fanning's 22-year-old record of 18 goals.

Perhaps in a lapse of concentration or nerves, McKenna proceeded to kick 3 behinds in a row before finally kicking another 2 goals in time-on to finish with 16.4 for the day.

"I led out to the ball in the last quarter to Wayne Richardson...The crowd was aware of the league record (I didn't give a stuff about records) ...and I got too close to him, so he had a shot and missed. He did the right thing, because I was too close to him,

and the whole Collingwood crowd booed him!"

When McKenna played his final season, with Carlton in 1977, he had kicked 874 goals from 191 games at an average of 4.58, putting him in the top five for the highest average of goals per game, higher than Coventry, Ablett Sr, Wade and Pratt.

After a stagnant start to his career at Collingwood, McKenna became extraordinarily consistent, and didn't have a goalless game over a five-year span starting from Round 1 1968 to Round 3 1974. 120 consecutive games! (Still a V/AFL record).

At the peak of his career, McKenna was the most notable footballer in Victoria thanks to his bubbly pop-star career, his Beatles mop, and his dead-eye right foot. Every young Collingwood fan had their full-forward's number six on the back of their jumper, and often they would flood the field (even during games) to touch McKenna. If social media existed in the 1970s, McKenna would have more followers than Dustin Martin, Bailey Smith and Lance Franklin himself.

Below is a list of players to play the most games kicking at least one goal.

Games	Player	Teams	Period
121	Peter McKenna	CW/CA	1968-1974
114	Tony Lockett	SK/SY	1993-2002
98	Gordon Coventry	CW	1932-1937
97	Dick Lee	CW	1910-1918
90	Doug Wade	GE/NM	1971-1975
80	Bill Mohr	SK	1933-1938

Doug Wade

Capable on his day of taking towering marks and snapping goals from the bottom of the pack, Douglas G. Wade is the most underrated 1,000-goal member.

Across his 267-game career, Wade kicked 1,057 screw punts through the big sticks; he did not attempt a drop punt for goal across his 15 years with Geelong and North Melbourne.

Able to kick more than 60m regularly with his famous screw punt, Wade's record at Kardinia Park, which was practically a wind tunnel in the 1960s, was fantastic, with 413 goals in 99 games at an average of 4.17.

After kicking 5 goals in a practice match for Melbourne, Geelong coach Bobby Davis drove straight to Wade's household and signed him up, with parental permission of course.

Wade kicked 51 goals from 16 games in his first season and won his first Coleman Medal the very next year, in 1962, at 20 years old. (Only eight footballers have won a Coleman Medal under the age of 21, some of those names include Lance Franklin, Tony Lockett, John Coleman, and Dick Lee who had three before his 21st birthday).

Wade's crème de la crème season was 1969.

After Hudson in 1968 became the first player since John Coleman to kick 100 goals in a season, Wade did it the following year, kicking 122 goals and 75 behinds from 21 games. The Cats spearhead was unstoppable at the goal-mouth and averaged seven goals a game for the entire month of May. After kicking 8.5 in a 12-point loss to St. Kilda in Round 15, Wade went into their next clash against Footscray needing 11 goals to reach the magical 100-mark.

Hudson and Wade, up until that point in the season, were going toe to toe. After 11 rounds, Hudson had 65 goals, while Wade had 64, and by Round 15, Wade was 4 goals in front of the Hawthorn forward with 89 goals.

Round 16 was split over two weeks, with Hudson kicking 9.0 on 26 July against Melbourne, pushing him to 94 for the season, many tipping him as the first centurion of the 1969 season.

A strange event occurred at Kardinia Park in the second half of the split round. After a tight first half with the Cats leading by 20 points, Wade had only kicked one goal for the match and was being beaten by his opponent Gary Merrington.

Geelong directed their attack to Wade in the second half, and the floodgates opened. The Cats kicked 15-10-100 in the second half, with Wade kicking 10 off his own boot.

In 1973, the VFL introduced a 10-year rule whereby players with 10 years' service at their original club could move to another club of their choice.

Attracted by a move to Melbourne, plus a $20,000 sign-on fee and $10,000 salary, Wade moved to Arden Street (North Melbourne) to join Ron Barassi, finishing the 1973 season with 74 goals.

The following season, at the ripe old age of 32, Wade kicked 103 goals from 24 games, winning his fourth and last Coleman Medal to become the second forward in history after Jack Titus in 1940 to kick 100 goals without kicking a bag of 10 or more in a game.

Wade's longevity was admirable when footballers were still working full-time jobs. He won Coleman Medals 12 years and 4389 days apart.

Geoff Blython and Larry Donohue are two forgotten centurions.

The bespectacled Geoff Blethyn became the first Essendon forward after the great John Coleman to kick 100. As one of the first footballers to wear glasses on the field, Blethyn kicked 4.0 at only 17 years of age in front of 116,000 screaming fans in the 1968 Grand

Final with only one contact lens!

He started the 1972 season on fire with 7.5 against Footscray, 7.3 against Richmond, 7.8 against Geelong and 7.2 against Carlton in the first five weeks. When Blethyn kicked 11.3 in a 34-point loss to Footscray, the Bombers forward now had 61 goals from 12 games and the journos started to talk about the century.

Blethyn powered on kicking his 100th goal in empathic style with a 65m torpedo. His reward was being slobbered on by the police horse who was ridden close as protection from the delirious crowd that rushed onto the oval the celebrate the achievement.

The following year the young bespectacled star moved to Western Australia to play with Claremont in the WAFL.

Just 21 years old, Larry Donohue was a man mountain at 196cm and 97kg. After 22 games from his first three years, Donohue was moved from a centre-half-forward/ruck to a stay-at-home full-forward at the start of the 1972 season.

The big man was consistent and accurate, kicking 7.1 against South Melbourne in Round 1, 8.0 from eight kicks against Melbourne in Round 10, 9.6 from 19 kicks and 16 marks against South Melbourne later in Round 12. Heading into the final round of the home-and-away season needing 5 goals to reach the ton, Donohue had a chance to join George Moloney and Doug Wade when he lined up just outside 50 in the last quarter. Donohue set sail for home with his notorious long kick, with the Cattery crowd already starting to run on to the field. They believed it was a goal, and so did Donohue.

The only person that didn't think it was a goal was the goal umpire. The Sherrin had travelled over the posts. It didn't deter Donohue, who kicked his 100th with the first goal of the elimination final the following week. The Cats forward played 105 games and kicked 339 goals at 3.23.

THE HOLY TRINITY OF THE 90s

Good things always come in threes. Tennis has seen the most dominant trio in sporting history with Roger Federer, Rafael Nadal, and Novak Djokovic. The Chicago Bulls had Michael Jordan, Scottie Pippen, and Dennis Rodman during their golden era. Harry Potter had Harry, Ron, and Hermione, and the '90s had Tony Lockett, Jason Dunstall, and Gary Ablett Sr.

This fabulous goal-scoring trio emerged in the late '80s and left their mark.

Before these three, we saw some great full forwards come and go, but none left a bigger imprint.

"Disco" Michael Roach was a sight to behold for Richmond supporters, soaring high above packs and winning back-to-back Coleman Medals in 1980 and 1981 with 112 goals during the Tigers Premiership year in 1980.

Footscray, although unsuccessful during this period, had some fantastic forwards such as Kelvin Templeton who kicked 118 goals from full-forward in 1978, including 15.9 against St. Kilda, and won a Brownlow at centre-half-forward in 1980, kicking 82 goals.

The Bulldogs also had Sandgroper Simon Beasley, who kicked 575 goals at 3.73 for Footscray during the 80s. Super-Boot Bernie Quinlan, after 177 games at the Western Oval, moved over to Fitzroy and became a cult legend, winning two Coleman Medals and a Brownlow on his way to 510 goals at 3.33 during the decade.

No-one kicked the ball as far as Quinlan. Tall and athletic, Quinlan could play all over the field and kick running torpedoes from the wing of Princess Park where the nomadic Lions found

themselves through this period. He was practically a Buddy prototype. Channel Seven's Brian Taylor could turn it on in his playing days when he wanted to, kicking 518 goals at 3.87 across the '80s, including passing the 100 mark in 1986 for Collingwood.

We also saw the quintessential showman Warwick Capper kick 100 goals in 1986 and take the mark of the year. He burnt the candle at both ends on and off the field, and turned his football career into television shows, pop singles and even spreads in Playboy magazine, and still kicked 340 goals at 3.21 across his lively career.

Between 1987 to 1996, the Holy Trinity were at their damaging best. Dunstall kicked 100 goals in a season six times, Lockett passed 100 five times, and Ablett did it three years on the trot between 1993 to 1995.

Player	Games	Goals	Ave	Accuracy	7+ goals	10+ goals	A/A FF
Dunstall	210	1066	5.08	65.76	36	16	3
Lockett	153	894	5.84	69.46	37	19	3
Ablett Sr	192	841	4.38	61.21	29	12	3

Across these 10 years, each of the Holy Trinity was named All-Australian full-forward three different times. A strange coincidence.

What I find interesting about the above chart is Dunstall's consistency, averaging 21 games and 106 goals a season. Lockett's accuracy of 69.46% and the fact he kicked 7 or more goals in a game in 43.14% of the matches he played across this time is remarkable, as are the feats of the freakishly talented Ablett who only spent four of the 10 seasons as a stay-at-home full forward. Each of these greats had their own little something that made them amazing.

Gary Ablett Sr

Older than the other two, Ablett started at Hawthorn in 1982 as a 21-year-old yet struggled to settle down in the city and moved up north at season-end to play with Myrtleford in the Ovens and Murray Football League.

In what was one of the greatest recruiting pushes in modern footy, Geelong convinced the young star of the prospect of playing League football away from the city life and spent $60,000 on a clearance to get him down to Kardinia Park.

With a couple of speed humps on the way, Ablett paid back the Cats' board and supporter base in spades. He played on instinct and natural ability, becoming one of the greatest wingmen/half-forwards ever seen.

After nine games on the wing for Geelong in 1984, Ablett was selected in the Victorian Team to play Western Australia at Subiaco Oval. Playing on the half-forward flank he kicked 8 goals.

Ablett had a knack of making the burliest bloke at the pub giggle like a little child when he had the ball in his hands. Able to kick close to 70m with a drop punt, Ablett could turn on a dime and have a shot on goal from anywhere. If he was born in the United States, he could have been a wide-receiver pro-ball champion.

Ablett's efforts in the 1989 VFL season were something to behold. Rotating between the wing and half-forward line, Ablett produced one of the greatest performances ever seen in Round 9, kicking 14 goals from 30 disposals and 14 marks against Richmond. To prove it was no fluke, in sluggish conditions at the MCG the next week, Ablett had 28 disposals and kicked 7 goals 6 behinds, including the goal of the year.

When the 1989 finals kicked off, Ablett produced one of the greatest months of football ever seen. Although Geelong was at their dominant best heading into the finals (the Cats averaged 133 points a game), they were humbled by a hungrier Essendon side and walloped to the tune of 76 points in the series opener. Not one to be put off, Ablett turned on the jets and kicked 24 goals in the remaining three finals.

A 170-point turnaround on the back of Ablett's prowess saw the Cats easily dismantle the Bombers. Ablett was on fire from the first bounce, setting the tone early with 12 kicks and 4 goals before setting up three more as Geelong had 14 majors on the board at half-time; he finished the game with 8 goals.

The next week in perhaps the greatest game ever played, Geelong would take on the might of Hawthorn in front of 94,000 at the MCG. The Hawks also had an exceptional spearhead in Jason Dunstall, who had kicked 266 goals in the past two seasons.

The Hawks overpowered Geelong in the first half going into the half-time break with a 37-point lead. But Hawks coach Allan Jeans was well aware of the mercurial Ablett, who had kicked 4 goals on Scott McGuinness, and moved the ever-reliable Chris Langford on to the Geelong star for the second half. By the time Ablett out-manoeuvred Langford in the last quarter and kicked his 8th goal, the margin had been brought back down to 16 points and alarm bells started to ring.

With only 13 fit men on the field, the Hawks held on to win by six points in a fantastic shootout, 21-18-144 to 21-12-138. Ablett equalled Coventry's record of 9 goals in a Grand Final and was awarded the Norm Smith Medal.

After a disappointing 1990 season, Ablett famously announced his retirement at the start of the 1991 season yet was coerced to come back halfway through the season.

Retiring at 29 wouldn't have been a fitting end to one of the most gifted footballers in history. Ablett came back fitter and stronger in 1992, yet it was a move to full-forward by Cats coach Malcolm Blight that saw Ablett reach "God-like" levels.

In his first season playing out of the goal-square, Ablett reached 50 goals in six games (equalling Bob Pratt's record) and became the second-fastest player in history to reach 100 goals, in his 14th game.

Surprisingly Geelong missed out on the finals, yet Ablett finished with 124 goals from only 17 games, won the AFL MVP award (Leigh Matthews Trophy) and the AFLM Player of the Year Award. Kicking 10 or more goals in a game five times, Ablett's Round-6 performance against Essendon at the MCG was quite frankly, ridiculous. Geelong lost by 4 goals to Essendon 23-18-156 to 19-18-132, but it was the 31-year-old who carried Geelong like Atlas carrying the globe, dismantling four opponents (including a young James Hird) on his way to 14 goals, seven behinds – 91 points off his own boot. If only he kicked a little straighter. Ablett even went goalless in the last 10 minutes of the match!

Between 1993 to 1995, Ablett kicked 375 goals at 5.86, Dunstall kicked 290 goals at 5.09, and Lockett kicked 219 at 5.62 and kicked 516 goals after his 30th birthday. What a champion!

Jason Dunstall

Jason Dunstall was by far the most consistent full-forward during the '80s and '90s.

Although Lockett had the greater goal average and Ablett had a more freakish ability, the "Chief" fronted up season after season and produced results for the powerful Hawthorn side.

Dunstall's unselfishness in a dominant team was exemplified in the back-to-back club champion awards in Premiership seasons (1988 and 1989). In both those seasons, he also kicked 100 goals (132 and 138) and won the Coleman Medal, gaining

All-Australian honours as well. During the Hawks' dominant Premiership era between 1986 to 1991, Dunstall kicked 606 goals from 129 games at an average of 4.70. The next three seasons produced Dunstall's greatest output. Across this period, the Hawks relied on Dunstall more, and he became their greatest weapon kicking 369 goals at 5.86 a game across those three seasons, booting 36.68% of Hawthorn's goals.

1992 was Dunstall's crème de la crème year, with 343 disposals, 199 marks and 145 goals, 84 behinds. It's flabbergasting to think he didn't win the Brownlow, finishing second to Footscray's ruckman Scott Wynd by two votes.

At 27-years-of-age and at the peak of his powers, the Hawthorn full-forward had 343 disposals, 199 marks and kicked 145 goals, 84 behinds in 23 games.

Dunstall started the season with 12 goals against Geelong in Round 1, dismantling Cats defender Tim McGrath. On another sunny day at Waverley Park, Dunstall kicked a bag of nine against Collingwood in Round 6, playing on and defeating three opponents in Gary Pert, Rod McKeown and Mick Gayfer.

The next week however was Dunstall's pièce de resistance. The scoreboard read, Jason Dunstall 17-5-107 to Richmond 14-9-93. At the end of the first quarter, he had 6 goals to his name, having already played on two opponents (Jeff Hogg and Terry Keays), and by halftime he had 11. Well on track to breaking Fred Fanning's 1947 record of 18 goals, Dunstall's third and final opponent was rugged defender Scott Turner who was forced to implement interesting, niggling methods to curtail Dunstall.

Finishing the day with 17 goals, Dunstall also hit the post twice and famously looked for teammates in better positions when he was closing in on the record.

Since game statistics and fantasy points were calculated in

1965, no player has had a greater game. His stat-line is simply unbelievable: 25 kicks, 18 marks, 4 handballs, 17 goals, 5 behinds, 5 free kicks, 243 dream-team points.

With 55 goals from his first seven games, there was talk about Dunstall possibly breaking the 150-goal mark set by Pratt and Hudson.

On a rainy day at Kardinia Park, Dunstall passed the 100 mark with more than eight games left in the home-and-away season. Dunstall's chances of passing the record was impeded by a three-week period that saw him kick only 3 goals, including being held goalless by St. Kilda Captain Danny Frawley.

Dunstall responded the next week emphatically, kicking 38 goals in his last five games, including 12 goals 8 behinds against the Bombers and feasted on Richmond for the second time for the year, on his way to 27 disposals, 16 marks and kicking 12 goals, 6 behinds. Dunstall finished 5 goals short of the record, yet also kicked 84 behinds including 22 in his last four games. Hitting the scoreboard 229 times in a season, if Dunstall sharpened his accuracy only a fraction more, he'd have the goal-kicking record.

Dunstall kicked another 123 goals in 1993, finished third in the Brownlow yet was overlooked for All-Australian selection, with the selectors deciding to go with Ablett Sr who kicked 124 goals at 7.29 and Adelaide high-flyer Tony Modra who won the Coleman Medal with 129 goals at 5.61.

Dunstall's love for Hawthorn was unwavering. Named captain in 1995, the "Chief" showed he could still kick goals with a young side and finished the 1996 season with another century.

The once powerful Hawks were subject of talk about a possible merger with Melbourne and found themselves facing the Demons in the last round of the 1996 season. In what was labelled as the "Merger Game", many fans attended (63,196) believing that this could be the last time they saw their beloved team in action. Leading from the front, the captain kicked 10 goals, including his 100th for the season, as the Hawks won by a solitary point.

Tony Lockett

Every footballer, young or old, where it be on the footy field or in their own backyard, has at one time or another practiced the Tony Lockett set-shot routine.

For a man who was intimidating, volatile and temperamental, Lockett's routine was the opposite. It followed a slow concise build up with his eyes zoned in on the pigskin, arms close to his feet to minimise the drop of the ball, a perfect connection, and an effortless follow-through.

Tony Lockett was in every sense of the word a classical

footballer. At 191cm and close to 115kg, "Plugger" was the prototype modern full-forward.

An Imposing figure, Lockett moved around the forward line like a ballerina. He was deceptively quick off the lead and used his large frame to keep the ball away from his defenders.

He won his first club goal-kicking award at 18 and was a hero for many Saints fans, who often were left in bewilderment as big Tony defeated three opponents on the muddy Moorabbin deck game after game.

In 12 seasons at St. Kilda, Lockett was only on the winning side 68 times, and kicked 470 goals at 6.91 in those victories. Amazingly, Lockett had already kicked 657 goals and played 141 games before his first final, won a Brownlow Medal, the AFL MVP award and won two Coleman Medals.

Throughout his illustrious 281-game career, Lockett is statistically the greatest goal-kicker of all-time; 1,360 goals at a conversion rate of 70%, "Plugger" was the Robin Hood of archers.

A stat that must be seen to be believed is that Lockett has more goals in losses than fellow Coleman Medallists including Fraser Gehrig, Brian Taylor, John Longmire, John Peck and Malcolm Blight kicked in their careers. Across those 156 losses, they were by an average margin of 39.63 points, which is remarkable for Lockett to still kick 567 goals.

Player	TM	GL	GM	AV
Tony Lockett	SK/SY	567	156	3.63
Fraser Gehrig	WC/SK	549	260	2.11
Brian Taylor	RI/CW	527	140	3.76
John Longmire	NM	511	200	2.55
John Peck	HW	475	213	2.23
Malcolm Blight	NM	444	178	2.49

At the start of the 1989 season Lockett embarked on one of the greatest stretches of goal-kicking ever seen.

Over a 50-game period between Round 1, 1989 to Round 13, 1992, Lockett kicked 339 goals at an average of 6.78 per game. "Plugger" kicked 41.94% of St Kilda's total goals across this period. He kicked 24 bags of 7 or more goals.

To add another layer to this brilliance, 26 bags of seven or more have been kicked since 2018; that is 990 games of footy! Over a 50-game period, no footballer in history has kicked more than 339.

To truly put that into perspective, at the beginning of the 2023 season the North Melbourne team had kicked 435 goals in their last 50 games. Players to have also kicked 300 or more in a 50-game period are Peter McKenna 333 at 6.66, Peter Hudson 330 at 6.60, Bob Pratt 328 at 6.56, Jason Dunstall 316 at 6.32 and Gary Ablett Sr 300 at 6.00.

Lockett was at his damaging best when Ken Sheldon was coach of the Sainters between 1990-93.

Between 1988 to 1990, Lockett only played 31 games, yet it was his blistering start to the 1991 season and coaching from goalkicking legend and St. Kilda club manager Peter Hudson that saw "Plugger" play his best two back-to-back seasons, with St. Kilda also playing finals for the first time since 1973.

Lockett missed the first six games of the season with a cracked vertebra, yet it didn't stop him winning the Coleman Medal with 127 goals from only 17 games (Dunstall had 32 goals and Peter Sumich had 31 goals before Lockett played a game).

A 30-goal lead didn't mean anything to "Plugger" as he proceeded to kick 50 in his first six games including 12 against Adelaide, 10 against the Brisbane Bears and another 12 against Sydney in consecutive weeks.

By Round 15 Lockett was leading the Coleman Medal and was

the most in-form forward in the competition, kicking 13 against Carlton in Round 17, another 10 against Adelaide at Moorabbin Oval to bring up his century and finished the season with 11 against Sydney, and 9 goals 5 behinds in his first final, with the Saints losing by seven points to Geelong at Waverley Park in front of 63,796 spectators.

Another 132 goals and All-Australian honours for Lockett in 1992, including a St. Kilda club record of 15 goals against Sydney in Round 13, was followed by more injuries and suspension in 1993 and 1994.

Lockett had a fiery temper, which saw him suspended for a total of 23 matches across his career, and by 1994, he was tired of living in Melbourne and wanted to move.

Paving the way for the likes of Franklin, Lockett was coerced to move to Sydney and the rest, as they say, is history.

Who could forget that 16 goal-haul against Fitzroy in 1995, the behind after the siren with millions watching around Australia to send Sydney into their first Grand Final since the Bloodbath in 1945, and who could forget the moment at the SCG when he wobbled a drop punt through to break Gordon Coventry's record and kick his 1,300th goal?

Such was the goalkicking brilliance in the 1990s, five times a player kicked 100 or more in a season yet failed to win the Coleman Medal. Tony Lockett (1992, 1995) and Jason Dunstall (1993, 1996) did it twice, exemplifying their brilliance.

As Roger Federer, Rafael Nadal, and Novak Djokovic had an everlasting effect on Tennis, Lockett, Dunstall, and Ablett's effect on Australian Rules Football cannot be denied. Between 1987 to 1996, they were the three highest-profile full forwards in the competition. Across the decade of brilliance, the average of goals per game was 14.33, and the average score was 97.12.

TONY MODRA

Across the Western Highway, hailing from the Riverlands region in South Australia, Adelaide had unearthed a star in the making.

Tony Modra debuted at a relatively old age of 23 after kicking a mountain of goals in the Riverlands Football League and showing promising signs in the SANFL with West Adelaide Football Club.

Modra's career with the Adelaide Crows might not have reached the glorious heights he famously soared to on the field if it wasn't for an unfortunate injury to prolific SANFL full-forward Scott Hodges at the start of the 1993 season.

Hodges finished the 1992 season with 48 goals from 13 games, including 11.4 against Grand Finalists Geelong at Kardinia Park. Modra kicked 21 goals from eight games but neither full forward could get a solid run at it. Hodges had a fearsome reputation in the SANFL and was a Magarey Medallist after breaking the SANFL record in 1990 with 153 goals to go with the hallowed medal.

All that changed when Modra announced himself to the league with 10 goals against Richmond in the opening round of the 1993 season. By Round 8, when the Crows spearhead kicked 10.1 against North Melbourne in a two-point win, Modra had become the most recognisable person in South Australia.

Nicknamed "Godra", he was the Brad Pitt of full forwards. With his Hollywood look, muscular frame and perfect blonde hair, every young female fan adored their new goalkicking tyro.

In Round 16, Modra set a new goal-kicking record with 13.4 against Richmond and kicked his 100th for the season against Fitzroy in Round 19. He finished the home-and-away season with 119 goals (the fourth most in a season not to win the Coleman Medal) and kicked 129 for the entire season.

After Modra's brilliant season, the magnificent aerialist would kick 50 or more goals five times in a season, but never again achieved the 100-goal mark. Modra was awarded the Coleman Medal in 1997 with 81 goals but sadly missed out on a chance to win a Premiership with Adelaide, buckling his knee in the preliminary final against the Western Bulldogs.

He finished his career over in Western Australia and kicked 588 goals at 3.56 from his 165 AFL games.

Below is a list of most goals in a season to finish second in the Coleman Medal.

AV	GL	GM	Player	TM	Year
6.40	128	20	Peter McKenna	CW	1970
6.15	123	20	Tony Lockett	SK	1992
6.32	120	19	Peter Hudson	HW	1969
5.95	119	20	Tony Modra	AD	1993
5.85	117	20	Jason Dunstall	HW	1993
5.79	110	19	Tony Lockett	SY	1995
4.77	105	22	Geoff Blethlyn	ES	1972
6.38	102	16	Bob Pratt	SM	1933
4.59	101	22	Jason Dunstall	HW	1996
5.56	100	18	Gordon Coventry	CW	1934
4.54	100	22	Alex Jesualenko	CA	1970

Matthew Lloyd 2000 and 2001

The next decade saw a decline in team scoring, dropping to 92.57 per game, with the lowest average of 90 in 2006. During this decade, Matthew Lloyd reigned supreme with 742 goals at 3.79 across 196 games, winning three Coleman Medals.

Accuracy was synonymous with Lloyd's name, and his set-shot routine became famous. At the top of his mark, Lloyd would pull his socks up without hesitation, tossing a blade of grass in the air to bring his heart rate down. His trusty left foot rarely let him down within the 50m arc.

A scoring renaissance occurred in 2000 with the average per game increasing to 101. Teams including Essendon, Carlton, Melbourne, and the Brisbane Lions all scored more than 2,500 points for the season. Essendon had statistically the greatest season ever winning 24 games and scoring 3,274 points at an average of 130.96. Matthew Lloyd was the focal point of this dominant forward line with 109 goals.

Lloyd's consistency was remarkable, playing in all 25 games, and kicking 5 goals or more in 10 of them. The next season was Lloyd's best, when he kicked 105 goals in only 21 games at an average of 5 goals a game.

One game that stands out was his 10.4 performance against West Coast in Round 6. The Essendon sharpshooter went scoreless in the first quarter, before kicking 4 goals in six minutes in the third quarter. Lloyd finished both home-and-away seasons with 94 and 96 goals, proving how consistent you must be to kick 100.

Fraser Gehrig 2004

In 2004, Lloyd finished the home-and-away season with 89 goals yet was snuffed out by the barest of margins by 28-year-old makeshift Saints full-forward Fraser Gehrig, who was trialled as a key forward in the second half of 2003 and made the goal-square his home in 2004.

Gehrig's large frame (109kg playing weight) and versatility saw him play various roles at West Coast and St. Kilda.

Initially used as a full-back when he joined the Saints in 2001, Gehrig enjoyed his time as a full-forward kicking 103 goals and 39 behinds, as the accurate Saints pilled on 370 goals and 223 behinds for the home-and-away Season, including a stretch of 78 goals from Round 8 to 10.

By Round 10, Gehrig had 50 goals to his name and was well on his way to 100 goals. Two goalless games were followed by a bag of 10 against North Melbourne, 8 against Essendon and 13 in three finals saw Gehrig pass the century mark in the preliminary final at Football Park against Port Adelaide.

In an unusual circumstance, St. Kilda had the momentum in the first quarter when Gehrig lined up for his 100th goal. Many Saints players, including former captain Nick Riewoldt, pleaded with their fans not to run onto the field when Gehrig passed the mark.

As fate would have it, Gehrig became the third Saints forward after Bill Mohr and Tony Lockett to pass the century mark, and the Saints lost by six points, thanks to a Gavin Wanganeen blinder from the boundary.

Lance "Buddy" Franklin, 2008

The defining age for some of the game's greats has been 21.

Keith Greig won his first Brownlow Medal at 21years and 315 days in 1973 for North Melbourne. Michael Voss won Brisbane's first Brownlow Medal in 1996 at 21 years and 73 days. Chris Judd after only 68 games in the AFL announced himself as the best midfielder in Australia with a Brownlow Medal at 21 years and 12 days in 2004, and Tony Lockett became the first full-forward to win the coveted medal and Coleman Medal double at 21 years and 195 days in 1987.

Lance Franklin is the fifth youngest centurion in V/AFL history and is the youngest centurion since Lockett in 1987, who was 162 days older than Franklin.

The similarities between Lockett's 1987 and Franklin's 2008

Year	Age	Day	Player	TM
1949	20	305	John Coleman	ES
1933	21	2	Bob Pratt	SM
1987	21	52	Tony Lockett	SK
1976	21	135	Larry Donohue	GE
2008	21	213	Lance Franklin	HW
1950	21	269	John Coleman	ES
1972	21	303	Geoff Blethyn	ES
1938	21	308	Ron Todd	CW
1980	21	312	Michael Roach	RI
1978	21	316	Kelvin Templeton	FO
1934	21	338	Bob Pratt	SM

seasons are uncanny. Not only were they similar ages, but they also polled 20 Brownlow Votes each for the season. Lockett averaged more goals a game with 5.32, but Franklin averaged more disposals with 15.32.

Player	TM	YR	KI	MK	HB	DA	GL	BH	Vote AV
Tony Lockett	SK	1987	10.27	7.45	2.23	12.5	5.32	2.36	0.91
Lance Franklin	HW	2008	12.32	6.32	3.00	15.32	4.52	3.52	0.91

After announcing himself as the next big star in the AFL with a 7-goal performance against Adelaide in the 2007 elimination final, Buddy was primed and ready to detonate in 2008.

Franklin showed glimpses of his power up forward with 15 goals in consecutive weeks in 2007, but 2008 was the season when Buddy consistently hit the scoreboard.

In front of 30,019 under lights, Franklin lit up the Gabba in Round 5 with a commanding performance.

The scoreboard see-sawed for the first three quarters, with the lead changing eight times during the game. The Hawks lead by two points heading into the last quarter.

Franklin turned on the jets in the last quarter showing his agility as a tall forward who could play small, with a dribbler goal from the boundary and a 55m bomb from the opposite pocket (for a left foot kick) to finish with 8.6 in a best-on-ground performance.

It was not a season without blemishes, though; Buddy kicked 1.7 the following week against Richmond but proved again that he loved to flourish on the big stage, kicking 6 second-half goals against Collingwood the week after in front of 76,048 at the MCG.

By the season's halfway mark, the stars were aligning for the Hawks who were sitting at the top of the ladder with Geelong. Everything was sailing smoothly until Franklin sent journalists into a frenzy with questions surrounding his party-boy persona after an altercation at a nightclub.

Buddy responded as all superstars do, kicking 9.5 against Essendon in front of a packed house at the Docklands. By Round 11, the goalkicking dynamo had kicked 59 goals and 38 behinds.

Returning from the bye with a top-four clash against Sydney at the MCG, Franklin's inaccuracy was a talking point, with the forward kicking 4.7 from 14 shots on goal (two out on the full, one didn't make the distance).

After 15 rounds, Buddy averaged 4.67 goals and 3.73 behinds a game. The Hawks' biggest test came in Round 17 against Geelong, who were 15-1 at the MCG in front of a packed house of 86,179. Hawthorn would eventually go down by 11 points but were not embarrassed by the mighty Geelong side.

Franklin was a headache up forward, kicking 4.5 on Cats greats Matthew Scarlett and Andrew Mackie. Two prolific weeks followed with best-on-ground performances against a Nick Maxwell-led Collingwood with 8.6 and 6.1 against the Lions in Tasmania in Shane Crawford's 300th game. Franklin had kicked 91 goals with three games left in the season.

Franklin kicked 7.11 over the next two weeks, with champion West Coast defender Darren Glass denying him the chance of kicking his 100th in front of a home WA crowd. Franklin now needed 2 goals in the final home-and-away round against Carlton to chase the illusive milestone.

Regarded as the "shoot-out at the Dome", mercurial Carlton forward Brendan Fevola also needed 8 goals to become a centurion. With talk of the athletic Jarrad Waite lining up on Franklin, the commentary box was shocked when Brett Ratten sent 24-gamer

Paul Bower to mind the explosive Buddy.

Carlton had the momentum in the first quarter but failed to capitalise, with Fevola missing the goals three times (Fevola would go on to kick another 7 goals in the second half, falling agonisingly short of the 100 mark).* The Hawks were more proficient in front of the sticks, with Franklin calmly moving to 99 with a set shot. A minute later, the electrifying Cyril Rioli found the Sherrin on the half-forward flank and chipped the ball over to Franklin for the historical moment, with Channel 10 commentator and Hawks fanatic Stephen Quartermain capturing the iconic moment on television.

"There's the security guards, they are lining up by the dozens, I don't think it's going to be enough."

"In he comes on 99 goals... LANCE FRANKLIN JOINS THE 100 CLUB and people power has spoken... out they come by the thousands. Just the 28th man in 150 years of AFL to reach the 100."

Franklin became the 28th footballer to kick 100 goals in a season and the first First Nations Australian to kick 100 goals in the V/AFL, breaking Jeff Farmer's 2000 record of 76 in round 17.

Franklin became the second state league First Nations Australian to kick 100 goals, joining East Fremantle's Kevin Taylor, who kicked 102 goals 64 behinds in 1979 playing as a rover in the WAFL. It is also worth noting that Dennis Dunne kicked 128 goals in the 1985/86 season for St. Marys in the Northern Territory

Football League. Franklin had become the most marketable footballer in Australia, with Channel 10 boundary rider Mark Howard saying, "It's like you're Mick Jagger!"

It is football folklore that, for no reason other than a competitive hubris, Alaistair Clarkson and his Hawthorn players refused to let anyone else share the spotlight with Franklin. More than 10 goals up at the time Clarkson flooded the Carlton forward line in a bid to thwart Fevola's 100- goal charge. He finished on 99. Fevola was quoted as saying at the time, "Give me the ball guys, you've already won, honestly." Post-game, an unrepentant Clarkson only said;

"Fevola had his chances."

Franklin and the Hawks knew they had bigger fish to fry as they turned their eyes towards a qualifying final clash, against a Western Bulldogs outfit that had the Hawks' measure in their Round 10 clash in Launceston.

The Bulldogs, with a strong defence featuring Brian Lake (Franklin's future premiership teammate and 2013 Norm Smith Medallist) and Dale Morris. Still, they knew they had their work cut out with Franklin, who had produced topsy-turvy results in their last three encounters, kicking 6.1, 2.11 and 5.0.

Hawthorn burst out of the gate in the first quarter, but the second-quarter blitz of 6.7-43 had the crowd in raptures. By the 19th minute mark of the second quarter, Franklin had kicked 5 of the Hawks' 8 goals and proved he was more than just a key position forward and he could also damage you when the ball hit the ground.

Franklin's first goal was a crumb after he spoiled the ball to the ground, his second goal was kicked from the goal-square with Ryan

Hargraves hanging off him, and his third goal came after he was knocked to the ground by Brian Lake, recovered his feet to smother Lake's handball, danced around another hapless defender and snapped from 35m. His first set-shot goal was his fifth for the night, and his next two were quintessential Buddy, using his explosive pace and power to kick goals 10 rows back from inside the 50m arc.

When Franklin split the pack open and ran into the goals for his 8th, he equalled the Hawthorn finals record set by fellow number 23, Dermott Brereton in the 1985 Grand Final and Michael Moncrieff, who kicked 8.1 in the 1978 qualifying final.

After a comfortable 51-point victory over the Bulldogs and a 54-point win over St. Kilda in the preliminary final, the Hawks faced off against a Geelong side that had only lost one game for the entire season.

In an enthralling contest in front of 100,012 fans (the highest crowd for a Grand Final since 1986, when Hawthorn defeated Carlton by 42 points in front of 101,861), the Hawks never let the heavily favoured Cats outfit use their free-flowing game style after quarter-time, Geelong putting 11 consecutive behinds (two were rushed) on the board in 33 minutes of football.

Buddy kicked his first for the game to give the Hawks a two-point lead, and the Cats' hopes were finally dashed in a five-minute patch of football in the third quarter when veteran recruit Stuart Dew kicked two fantastic goals and set up another two in a Grand Final cameo that will go down in footy folklore.

Buddy iced the game in the last quarter, kicking his 113th goal for the season.

Jarryd Roughead also kicked 2 goals that day, taking his 2008 tally to 75, finishing sixth in the home-and-away season with 66.

Franklin and Roughead's one-two-punch combo went a long way to Hawthorn's success in 2008. Buddy won the Coleman, Hawthorn's best and fairest honours, and finished third in the Brownlow Medal. Roughead had been picked three spots ahead of Franklin in the 2004 National Draft and was a perfect foil for the star forward.

Below is a list of teammates to kick 50 or more in a season

Year	TM	GL Total	Player	GL	Player	GL	Premier ship
1977	HW	201	Peter Hudson	110	Leigh Matthews	91	no
1980	RI	196	Michael Roach	112	Kevin Bartlett	84	yes
2008	HW	188	Lance Franklin	113	Jarryd Roughead	75	yes
1938	CW	185	Ron Todd	120	Des Fothergill	65	no
1993	HW	174	Jason Dunstall	123	Paul Hudson	51	no
1970	CA	170	Alex Jesaulenko	115	Syd Jackson	55	yes
2004	SK	170	Fraser Gehrig	103	Nick Riewoldt	67	no
1976	HW	168	Michael Moncrieff	97	Leigh Matthews	71	yes
1983	FI	167	Bernie Quinlan	116	Mick Conlan	51	no
2000	ES	166	Matthew Lloyd	109	Scott Lucas	57	yes
1971	GE	161	Doug Wade	94	Bill Ryan	67	no
1978	HW	161	Michael Moncrieff	90	Leigh Matthews	71	yes
1987	HW	158	Jason Dunstall	94	Dermott Brereton	64	no
1984	FI	156	Bernie Quinlan	105	Mick Conlan	51	no
1985	FO	156	Simon Beasley	101	Les Bamblett	55	no
1935	SM	155	Bob Pratt	103	Roy Moore	52	no
1982	ME	153	Gerard Healy	77	Mark Jackson	76	no
1992	GE	151	Bill Brownless	79	Gary Ablett Sr	71	no
1932	CA	150	Harry Vallance	97	Mickey Crisp	53	no
1989	GE	150	Gary Ablett Sr	87	Gavin Excell	63	no
1940	RI	150	Jack Titus	100	Dick Harris	50	no

Since that magical 100th goal on the 30 August 2008, Franklin's career has stood the test of timeand Buddy has proven himself the greatest forward of the modern era.

With three more Coleman Medals, seven more All-Australians, and 2 goals of the year, Franklin's longevity for someone who's 199cm is remarkable.

Footy lovers will take a long time to digest the magnitude of

1,000 goals in the AFL era, and it is a testament to Franklin's greatness.

Player	TM	GM	GL	AV
Lance Franklin	HW/SY	263	822	3.13
Jack Riewoldt	RI	300	730	2.43
Tom Hawkins	GE	308	707	2.3
Josh Kennedy	WC	264	705	2.67
Eddie Betts	CA/AD	275	555	2.02
Taylor Walker	AD	238	536	2.25
Jeremy Cameron	GW/GE	210	531	2.53
Jack Darling	WC	257	484	1.88
Luke Breust	HW	260	481	1.85
Jarryd Roughead	HW	203	459	2.26
Tom Lynch	GC/RI	212	447	2.11
Jack Gunston	AD/HW	225	430	1.91
Nick Riewoldt	SK	182	411	2.26

BUDDY BRILLIANT

Buddy Franklin has been something special on the football field, without question. No one kicks 100 goals in a season or 1,000 over a career without a healthy dose of X factor.

Think of Lockett (1,360 career goals), Dunstall (1,264), Ablett (1,031), Coventry (1,294) and Wade (1,057).

Then there's Buddy.

He's dazzled and dazed fans and opponents alike over 18 seasons at two clubs.

His goal-scoring career has produced many magic moments, probably none better than an effort on the hallowed MCG against Essendon in 2010.

Long-time Hawthorn supporters had no hesitation naming it his best. In fact, there were 2 goals by Buddy that day that caught the eye. Fans will long remember both.

David Withington, a 53-year Hawthorn member, and one-time "Hawk Talk" newsletter editor says: "No.1 would have to be his two freakish running and bouncing goals from the boundary line in the same game against Essendon at the MCG.

"Watching the first one was exhilarating enough, but you felt there could have been a bit of luck involved. Then when he repeated the feat a short time later in amazingly similar circumstances you put aside any thoughts of luck and knew you were simply watching a freak at work. It left us all breathless with amazement.

"The TV shots of his hapless opponent (Cale Hooker, who went on to be a very good player) chasing in vain as Buddy bounced his way around the boundary line are seared in my memory.

"A close No.2 would be his goal from outside 50 in the dying seconds to win the elimination final against Adelaide at Docklands in 2007, his and most of his teammates' first final. We were seated directly behind him and when he turned and triumphantly saluted the crowd everyone knew instantly that a superstar had been unleashed in that moment. And we were right (he'd kicked 7 goals). The following season Buddy kicked well over 100 goals and our young team of stars upset Geelong in the Grand Final."

"Wonderful memories."

Another Hawthorn Member, John Payne (now in his mid 60s), agreed with the choice: "I have been a member since age 7 and have seen some unbelievable Hawthorn players along the journey but Buddy is the best with only Cyril Rioli coming close by comparison.

"My memory of the second goal (in particular) was sitting on the opposite side of the ground in the Southern Stand and watching the Hawks fans behind the fence in the Olympic Stand come to their feet as he bounced the ball and ran past them along the boundary line. It was like a fan opening up. And the hair on my neck was standing up when the goal was kicked. I will never forget it.

"YouTube shows his best 23, just some of the most unbelievable goals ever seen in our game. He was THE best... a freak."

Buddy kicked the Goal of the Year in 2010.

It is Round 13. The Hawks are in a bruising struggle with Essendon at a packed MCG on a Friday night. Scores are level early in the final quarter.

Enter Buddy Franklin with two magical dashes down the wing for goal.

First, he charges towards a vacant goal square at the Punt Road end. He breaks clear of Essendon's Mark McVeigh, takes three bounces and dribbles a low goal through the posts.

No doubt, a goal of the year contender. But Buddy wasn't done.

Just minutes later he was hurtling down the wing again.

This time, he contests a mark with Essendon opponent Cale Hooker, regathers the ball when it tips over their heads, plays on after advantage was paid to him, and takes three more bounces (almost spilling one) and is forced closer to the boundary line, still homing in on the goal posts. Essendon defender Jarrod Atkinson, in his final AFL game, sprints into the goal square to try to save the day.

Can Buddy dribble through another goal? No.

He puts his super left boot to the ball and slots it through the goal posts from along the boundary line 50m out. Goal of the Year. Possibly even the two best goals of the year "back-to-back" as one commentator put it.

Over to 3AW commentary (Tony Leonard): "Franklin has to go again. He gets under the ball. Left his man there. It was Hooker. He is 70 metres out from goal. He has had two bounces. No-one's in the goal square. Hooker can't catch him. Three bounces. Keeps it low. (screaming, words inaudible). He's kicked the two best goals of the year back-to-back, Lance Franklin. You will not see a better goal this year."

The feat was made more amazing by the fact that as a left-foot kicker, he was close to the boundary line and the angle much tighter than for a right-footer.

We didn't see better that year. It **was** Goal of the Year. And fans won't forget it, nor the one kicked just minutes before it either.

Cale Hooker probably still has nightmares about that day. He said in an interview he hates talking about what became famous as "The Chase."

But he also laughs about it.

"After Buddy moved to Sydney I thought they'd stop showing the footage," he said. "But they still manage to sneak it on."

At least Hooker went on to be recognised as one of the top

defenders in the game at that time chalking up his 100th game in 2014. He retired in 2019 after 14-year, 219-game career with the Essendon Bombers.

While his 2010 effort is considered his best, Buddy also was recognised in 2013 for Goal of the Year.

In Round 3 against Collingwood, Buddy crossed the centre square at speed to collect a handpass from Ben Stratton, then had to hurdle Stratton who was going to ground in a tackle. He put boot to ball from 75m out for a goal - "an MCG special from Buddy," as Bruce McAvaney described it in Channel 7 commentary.

AFL statistics show one of Buddy's strengths has been his ability to mark and play on; his percentage of goal-success in that facet is around 70%. Most of his goals come from set shots as you'd expect, but the success rate is just on 60%. It's a similar percentage for goals on the run and along the ground.

Despite some of his best goals coming from a long way out, his best success rate is from within 15m. No surprise there. He's pretty accurate from 15 to 30m as well, at about a 65% success rate. Most of his goals (more than 270) and behinds (more than 240) have come from 40 to 50m but at a goal-success rate of a bit over 50%. From outside 50m (around 190 goals) his success rate is just on 50%.

In career of 1,000- plus goals here are some more of Buddy's best, based on the preferences of fans:

- 2012, Round 10 vs. North Melbourne. A case of the effort more so than the goal itself. Franklin spilled the mark, recovered, turned and snapped. All as the siren sounded. It was one of 13 for the day.
- 2014, Round 13 vs. Port Adelaide. Nine minutes left on the clock and up just a point, Franklin marked on the forward flank, turned and seeing the goal mouth unprotected launched the ball from 70m out. He wasn't done putting the Power's hopes to bed. Just a few minutes later he scooped up a half volley on the 50m mark, baulked, ran around an opponent, then another and kicked truly for a 13-point lead.

- 2018, Round 3 vs. GWS. Buddy gathered the ball at half forward, fended off a defender, angled away from the goals, and fired off a goal from 70m out.
- 2012, Grand Final vs. Sydney. He couldn't get the Hawks over the line against the Swans but his performance highlight was a bomb from 70m that kept his side in the contest.
- 2011, Preliminary Final vs. Collingwood. Not on the winning side, but a class effort to finish the match. The ball went into the Hawks' forward line, and Franklin, chased by Chris Tarrant, headed towards the boundary line to send a dribbling ball through the goal posts. The Hawks briefly took the lead but Collingwood put them out right at the end.
- 2017, Round 22 v Adelaide. The Swans were just 11 points up at three-quarter-time and the Crows kicked 3 in a row to take the lead in what was to become a fairly see-sawing affair. Buddy had kept the Swans in the competition with three trademark touches of brilliance. For his first, 17 minutes into the game, the ball is heading his way and he nudges Alex Keath under it to get the possession and streak goalward. His 2nd goal also was a nightmare for Keath, who may have thought staying in cricket with the Adelaide Strikers would have been a better idea and who had made his debut with the Crows just two rounds earlier. Both goals were impressive but not the best; this was – the 30-year-old swoops on a loose ball on the left wing and sets off. Two bounces and Daniel Talia sees him disappearing down the ground and from a tight angle 40m out, he puts the ball through the posts. Sydney goes on to win by three points in Adelaide, even though the home side led by nine points with five minutes to go.
- 2017, Round 23 v. Carlton. Just a week after his efforts in Adelaide, Buddy produced his biggest haul as a Swan with 10

gaols, securing the Coleman Medal as leading goalkicker of the year. Going into the final round Buddy was 5 goals behind West Coast Eagle Josh Kennedy in goals for the year. Franklin booted 10.2, roving and snapping on his left to reach double figures with seven minutes to play in an 81-point win. It gave him a 5-goal lead over Kennedy, who managed just one goal in the Eagles' match the next day. Franklin collected his fourth Coleman Medal, and second as a Swan.

Bruce McAvaney from Channel 7 summed it up: "He is the Usain Bolt of football."

In a career of more than 1,000 goals there are probably many others that could have been mentioned. His career-high "bag" was 13 goals, for Hawthorn against the North Melbourne Kangaroos. He may have gone goalless in his debut, for Hawthorn against the Swans back in 2004, but he buttered up the very next week with three against Richmond. His career was under way.

He scored 8 goals in each of seven other games in his career. By the end of the 2022 season, he had kicked 6 or more goals in 34 of his games. He had scored 79 goals against Essendon (his most against all clubs) up to 2023 so it would not only be Hooker who had nightmares. Nobody has kicked 100 goals in a season since Buddy did in 2008.

Buddy's abilities were well summed up by a sports media student from Canberra, Rory O Connor, writing for NowUC: "Buddy is one of very few players where you hold your breath every time the ball bounces near them because you know something special might happen. His left foot is something to behold, kicking goals from all sorts of places in a myriad of ways."

There have been some Buddy light moments

Adelaide forward Lachlan Murphy has revealed his hilarious first interaction with the champion.

Murphy, then appearing in just his 13th AFL game, was mistaken for a waterboy by Buddy in the middle of a match between the Crows and Swans.

"Sydney were having a shot for goal and Buddy was standing on the 50," Murphy told AFC Media.

"I went to stand behind him because I was star-struck, was three metres behind his shoulder.

"He turned around and indicated he wanted a drink of water, then realised I was a player and said 'oh, sorry mate'.

"He gave me a quick tap on the shoulder and ran off."

Murphy's Adelaide teammate Brodie Smith recalled another interaction, tweeting to Murphy: "Years back he told us he was on more (money) than our backline combined... we've since done the math... he was right."

In 2017 he was asked about retirement options, Buddy replied: "No doubt you are always thinking about what you are going to do when you finish football and you put some things in place."

Was study on the cards, for a new career perhaps? "I am not that big on the books to be honest with you."

There's also a Buddy Franklin parody song by Denis Carnahan called *5 Million Buck*s (The Buddy Franklin Song). It's been a YouTube hit.

The AFL developed a considerable following in the US when much of their domestic sport was shut down at the height of the Covid pandemic in 2022.

Former NFL star and more recently podcaster Pat McAfee became a fan, not just of AFL but of one player in particular, Buddy Franklin, and he didn't miss out on Buddy's 1,000th goal, thanks to tweets from an Australian.

"This is a once in a generation type thing to have happened, is what I was told by Aussies tweeting me," McAfee said. "Buddy f***ing Franklin. This guy, an absolute assassin with the footy.

"When the Sherrin is in his hand and he's running up and he's about to blast it, that son of a b***h could land it in a keyhole if he had to.

"He has different spins and curves and bends and magic.

"I couldn't help but get overwhelmed with joy for this guy.

"I'm just pumped for Buddy.

"This dude just did something awesome. That was amazing."

According to a News Ltd report, McAfee's co-host, AJ Hawk (also an ex-NFL player) praised Franklin for delivering under pressure as expectant fans begged him to reach 1,000 goals when he took a mark near goal late in the fourth quarter.

"You could see little kids sitting on the edge, everyone waiting to charge the field so he had to feel the momentum like, 'I better make this,'" Hawk said.

The Americans might not have understood the game all that well, but they grasped the significance of Buddy's goal number 1,000.

NUMBER 1,000

It is Friday night, 25 March 2022, and the Sydney Swans are at home on the Sydney Cricket Ground to the Geelong Cats in Round 2 of the AFL season.

It is a match with more hype than usual for so early in the season.

Buddy Franklin needs just 4 goals to reach a milestone that only five other players have achieved – 1,000 career goals.

The 36,578-strong Sydney crowd (probably including Cats supporters, too) is pumped in expectation. Officials and security are standing by as a ground invasion is on the cards.

The fans have eyes for only one person right from the first bounce of the night. Where's Buddy?

Buddy Franklin didn't get a touch until the 21-minute mark of the game, just before quarter-time. When he got is hands on the ball for the first time, he didn't miss for career goal number 997, from a tight angle.

The excitement was building. Security guards started to gather in greater numbers as the second quarter began. It turned into an anti-climax, as Buddy didn't land a shot in the second term, despite the Swans putting on a four-goal burst in just seven minutes to establish a 28-point lead.

Goal No, 978 came in the third quarter when Buddy won a free-kick from the Cats' Jack Harvey for a push in the back. Some said it was a dubious "free," but the result was a goal to Buddy. More security showed up.

There was even greater anticipation late in the third quarter, when Buddy slotted his third for the night and overall 999th with a trademark curling drop punt.

The siren to end the third quarter sounded and as the Swans players went into their huddle, fans began pressing towards the lower levels of the stands.

One quarter to go, and one more goal needed for No. 1,000. As commentators often say when scores are close in big events, the "tension is palpable."

Buddy only had to move to bring the crowd to its feet when the final quarter got under way.

There were boos around the ground when he was rested on the massage table briefly. He got a standing ovation when he stood up to take his place on the field again with 10 minutes to play, Sydney looking comfortably home over the off-target Cats.

One goal was still needed for the Buddy milestone.

Six minutes and 50 seconds remaining in the final term. Buddy is back on the field and the atmosphere is incredible.

Chad Warner, playing his first game, has the ball. Where's Buddy?

James Brayshaw on Channel 7: "Warner looks for No. 23. He's got him on short. And he's got it. Buddy... He's done it so many times. 999 goals Buddy Franklin. (Buddy steadies and walks in to kick, the ball's on its way). The legend becomes immortal."

Warner explained afterwards: "I had a lot of running room and I was about to bomb it over his head, but I saw him at the last minute and thought I have to go there don't I?

"I saw the goals and then I thought in the back of my head where's Lance, he was the only bloke I was thinking about and he had that much space. I just checked at the last minute and it was great, a pretty nice kick straight to him."

No problem for Buddy.

He marks 50m out and directly in front and goes back to line up his shot with 6 minutes 44 seconds on the Channel 7 clock.

The ball has barely left his left boot as the first of the fans come over the fence, followed by a wave flooding the ground.

Buddy has scored goal No. 1,000.

What ran through his mind as he lined up? He recalled later in an interview: "Well, I was just thinking, I better not miss this, I better not miss this. But the first couple of kicks I'd had, I was kicking well, so I was pretty confident. But there are always those doubts, especially when the pressure's on."

What followed was nothing short of pandemonium. It wasn't unexpected of course, but security was never going to be able to hold back the throng.

In the mayhem, Warner was celebrating along with the spectators and was heard to scream, "I f***ing kicked it to him!"

What wasn't immediately obvious was the "specky" a spectator took behind the goals as the ball sailed into the crowd off Buddy's boot. There was to be a sequel to that, with a happy ending.

Meanwhile, Buddy was mobbed. The fans came from everywhere around the ground.

The SCG playing surface was completely overrun. Commentator James Brayshaw: "I've never seen scenes like that at a sporting event anywhere."

Aerial vision showed almost all the playing surface completely covered by overjoyed fans, the number said to be 20,000. These were scenes not seen anywhere in the AFL since Swan Tony Lockett booted his 1,300th goal at the SCG on 6 June 1999.

It took more than half an hour for the crowd to disperse. There were still a few minutes of play to go, the Swans eventually defeating the Cats 17.5 (107) to 10.17 (77). Four goals to Buddy, and 5 to Isaac Heeney.

Buddy had 9 kicks, 7 marks (3 inside 50 m), 13 disposals, 8 uncontested possessions, a couple of clangers and one Brownlow vote for the match.

After the game ended, Warner and teammate Ollie Florent found themselves in their football gear outside the SCG, caught up in the departing (and celebrating) masses, having to negotiate their way back to the changerooms.

Buddy eventually was able to talk about his milestone.

"It was an amazing moment, it really was," he said. "A lot of hard work to get there. Been playing for 18 years. A lot of hard work to get there but I wouldn't be able to get there without having great teammates around me to provide those assists."

Asked his thoughts on being mobbed, he said: "I had the taste of Carlton Draught in my mouth from someone.

"It was an amazing moment. Something I will cherish forever."

Geelong coach Chris Scott: "It always had the potential to be Buddy's night, and Australian football in Sydney. We've got nothing but good things to say about the great man."

Swans coach John Longmire: "That was one of the most special moments you're going to get and look back on. We've just been able to watch one of the all-time greats go about his business. To be able to sit there and watch that tonight was pretty special."

Warner said afterwards Franklin's whereabouts had been on his mind in the final term, and he was proud of his role in creating a slice of history. He had high praise for Buddy.

"He's an amazing competitor. I reckon he's a big child at heart, he just loves playing with us young boys. Great for me obviously, my development and that.

"He's always got time for you which is amazing, especially a massive figure like him to hang out with him and all that stuff. He's an amazing bloke and an amazing father now as well."

While it was Buddy who entered the history books with his individual achievement, his opponents sang his praises as a team player. Port Adelaide fullback Tom Jonas said: "The thing you don't notice or doesn't get talked about with Buddy is how good a teammate he is.

“He is always bringing his other forwards into it. He’s really supportive of them, brings them into the game, communicates really strongly with them.

“He is not just a one-man band.”

Jonas had been assigned to play on Buddy several times and spoke about his presence.

“You’re always pretty nervous,” Jonas said.

“He cuts a serious figure. He has got an aura and a presence around him on the field... he has that strut and the chest puffed out.”

Richmond defender Dylan Grimes had similar sentiments.

“He has got the full package,” Grimes said. “He’s the hardest player I have ever played on because he’s got that speed, endurance and is an amazing finisher.

“He doesn’t need much of a chance to really damage a game, he’ll take it every time.”

Port Adelaide coach Ken Hinkley spoke about having to coach against Buddy. “He is almost impossible to plan for,” Hinkley said.

“He has got such a kit, the bag of stuff that he can do and draw on is so big and so wide and so exciting.

“You sit there trying to control and do your absolute best, but knowing the talent is very, very hard to stop.

“You hope he has an off day because his on days are unstoppable, just too good.”

Sadly for Buddy, Longmire, the Swans and their fans, the Cats were to extract their revenge for that Round 2 loss in no uncertain terms six months later in the Grand Final.

Buddy kicked 52 goals for the year, the 12th time he’d done so in 18 seasons (although he didn’t play in 2020).

Footnotes

1. The AFL, knowing that Buddy's 1,000th goal would come sometime during the season, had a plan. The Sherrin ball would be saved, mounted and prepared for a special presentation.

But there was always a chance the ball wouldn't get back to the AFL (or Buddy) when it was kicked into the crowd; some estimates put its value at $200,000.

Sure enough at the SCG on goal No. 1,000, it was snaffled by a fan, Alex Wheeler, who had been behind the goals. He didn't pass it back and made good his escape during the fan invasion that followed.

The Swans went public to try to regain it, offering incentives for its return, including other memorabilia signed by Franklin, involvement in a training session, and free memberships.

It may have worried Wheeler that the possibility of legal action was raised to secure its return. Anyway, he did the right thing on the following Monday and handed it over.

He said: "I had a few stubbies that night and went to the pub after but got paranoid that someone would get it from my house so went home pretty early. It was always my intention to get it back to the Swans and Buddy.

"It's going to be no good to me, I don't have a pool room to put it up in unfortunately. It was good to get in contact with the Swans and get it back to them."

He said he was encouraged by some people to sell the ball but felt that "wasn't right".

"I wanted to see it back at the SCG," he said.

It is now the prized possession of the man who last kicked it between the big sticks.

2. In a strange turn of events, Warner and teammate Ollie Florent found themselves on Driver Ave (outside the SCG on the west side of the ground) after Franklin's magical 1,000th goal. In a spur-of-the-moment decision to avoid the mass of spectators that had flooded on to the ground, the pair left the ground via the away-team's player race but were unable to get back into their dressing room. They had to go the long way down Driver Ave, much to the amusement of Swans' supporters.

"They were all just looking at us like, 'what the hell are you doing out here?' We were talking to each other to say, 'I can't believe we've still got a game going on right now — and we're outside'." Warner said to a staff writer from News.com.au.

Australian rules football is unique in its way that fans for more than 125 years have been allowed access to the surface, albeit with a far greater security presence in the modern age. Fans are still allowed to have a kick-to-kick with each other when the conditions suit the custodians of the fields. In fact, fans were going to access the field post-game 37 times across various grounds in the AFL during 2023. Crowd interaction has always been the most unique, and some may say most important, element in any sport across the globe; the spectators give the ground its atmosphere. But throughout the history of the V/AFL and VFA, it has resulted in some stressful moments.

In 1896 at Arden Street Oval, field umpire Jack Roberts was knocked to the ground and attacked by North Melbourne fans after some questionable decisions. Roberts was eventually saved by Collingwood defender and off-duty policeman Bill Proudfoot. In the early days of football in Victoria, spectators from clubs such as North Melbourne and Port Melbourne had a reputation for poor behaviour and hooliganism, which, apparently was the major reason they weren't accepted into the V/AFL in 1897.

Crowd interaction also has given us some of the most memorable moments in football, such as Lockett's 1,300th goal, Franklin's 100th goal in 2008, and his 1,000th goal in 2022. Watching a sea of spectators crash on to the field to celebrate is a truly remarkable moment in time.

Across the 127 years of the V/AFL, spectators have watched some of the greatest players kick their 100th goal for the season or 1,000th career goal, yet the crowd interaction with the milestone only started in 1969 when Doug Wade kicked his 100th goal against Footscray at Kardinia Park in round 16. Wade marked a drop-kick pass from Billy Goggin and was instantly subsumed by a tsunami of delirious fans without a security guard in sight.

Oddly enough the year before, Peter Hudson became the first to kick the 100 in 15 years, 11 months, and 5187 days, yet was only greeted by tap on the ass and congratulations from club captain Graham Arthur. Hawthorn's coach at the time John Kennedy Sr urged his troops to keep focused on the game and save their celebrations for when they were in the changerooms together. The year after Wade kicked his 100th goal against Footscray, Hudson kicked his second consecutive century and was mobbed by hundreds of excited Hawks fans.

"It was pretty scary, they were coming from all directions, and you're thinking 'what's going to happen when they all get here'... It's like driving down a dead-end street... Brian Crimmins (Peter Crimmins father) was the copper on the day and he got out

CELEBRATING 100 GOALS IN 1968.

really quickly, as did our trainers. They sort of created a wall around me to keep the people back a little"

PETER HUDSON

Since Wade and Hudson's magical moment in 1969, the sight of fans leaping over the fence and running onto the ground has become a staple in the V/AFL after a players have passed the magical 100 and 1,000 mark. It would be a terrible shame if this was lost to our great game.

3. While all the commotion surrounding Buddy's goal No. 1,000 two people made it to the centre square of the ground for a personal celebration of their own. They were there to drop the ashes of their recently deceased grandmother, a Swans supporter.

Joel Brown filmed as his sister Krystal Clayton made it to the middle and back, depositing the ashes on the centre square.

Their Nan, Edna Dixon, moved to the Central Coast from Melbourne in the early 80s and became a Swans fan.

"Nan passed away mid-last year aged 93," Mr Brown told the ABC. "She always said she wanted to do a coin toss on the SCG but she never got a chance."

THE FRANKLIN FILE

Lance (better known as Buddy) Franklin was born 30 January 1987 in in Perth, Western Australia.

Franklin is a proud First Nations Australian who has captained both the All-Australian team and the Indigenous All Stars.

His nickname "Buddy" was first used to differentiate him from his father, Lance Snr.

Career highlights:

- Twice AFL premiership player: 2008, 2013.
- Eight times All-Australian team: 2008, 2010, 2011, 2012, 2014, 2016, 2017, 2018.
- Four times Coleman Medal: 2008, 2011, 2014, 2017.
- Peter Crimmins (Hawthorn best and fairest) Medal: 2008.
- Six times Hawthorn leading goalkicker: 2007, 2008, 2009, 2010, 2011, 2012.
- Seven times Sydney leading goalkicker: 2014, 2015, 2016, 2017, 2018, 2021, 2022.
- Three times Brett Kirk Medal (best player in Sydney-GWS derby): 2017 (game 2), 2018 (game 2), 2021 (game 1).
- Twice Goodes–O'Loughlin Medal (best player in Swans match for Indigenous Round): 2017, 2022.
- Twice AFL Goal of the Year: 2010, 2013.
- AFL Rising Star nominee: 2005.

Heritage

Franklin's father, Lance Sr, lived in Melbourne and played hockey for Victoria before moving to Western Australia at the age of 21, later representing the state in field hockey. His mother, Ursula (née Kickett), is First Nations woman of the Noongar-Whadjuk. His sister, Bianca Giteau, played in the ANZ netball championship for the Adelaide Thunderbirds. She is married to former Wallaby Rugby Union international Matt Giteau. Former Australian Rules footballers Derek Kickett (West Perth, Claremont, Central District, North Melbourne, Essendon, Sydney) and Larry Kickett (East Perth, Claremont) are uncles. His cousins include former footballers Jeff Garlett (Melbourne/Carlton) and Dale Kickett (Fitzroy, West Coast, St Kilda, Essendon and Fremantle). Elijah Taylor (Sydney) is a second cousin. Byron Pickett (North Melbourne, Port Adelaide, Melbourne) is a nephew.

He wore a No. 67 jumper, as did several others, in the Sir Douglas Nicholls round in 2017 in commemoration of the 1967 referendum that voted to include First Nations Australians and Torres Strait Islanders in the Census.

Tattoos on his left arm are his way of celebrating his heritage, though not directly related to his Noongar-Whadjuk lineage. They are a random collection of images he found at a library; a First Nations elder, a kangaroo, a fire, a tree, a man sitting cross-legged playing the didgeridoo. Symbols of his "personal dreaming."

In an interview on *NITV* in June 2021 Tony Armstrong asked Buddy: "You're a Whadjuk-Noongar man, how immersed in your culture are you?" Buddy answered: "Super immersed, I think. No doubt, I am a proud Indigenous man. I'm a Noongar, I'm from Western Australia. Our culture is one of the longest living cultures in the world, so I'm super proud to be an Indigenous man. And we as a culture have been through a lot, and we still are going through a lot. So yeah, I'm just super proud."

Spouse – Jesinta Franklin

Lance Franklin married model, host, and beauty pageant queen Jesinta Campbell in November 2016, in Mount Wilson's Wildenstein Gardens in the Blue Mountains, west of Sydney. Jesinta wore a custom gown by famed bridal designer Vera Wang.

Jesinta was born on the Gold Coast, Queensland, 12 August 1991. She attended Aquinas College, a Catholic school in Southport. As a model she won the Miss Universe Australia title in 2010 and represented Australia in that year's Miss Universe pageant where she was second runner-up and won the Miss Congeniality award.

She has had modelling assignments with Jeep, Asics, Olay, Crown David Jones, and Tiffany & Co and has a global role for Seafolly swimwear.

Her hosting work began when she was a guest reporter for *The Morning Show*, reporting on topics related to fashion, entertainment, and pop culture. She also co-hosted he *Hot30 Countdown* with Matty Acton and appeared on *The Celebrity Apprentice Australia*.

Jesinta also wrote a book, *Live a Beautiful Life*, published in October 2016. She wrote about her favourite health and beauty tips, recipes, and other advice.

The lives of Jesinta and Buddy Franklin have fascinated Australian magazines ever since their first date.

Their meeting was a rich vein of glamour for the mags – beauty pageant queen and one of the best ever Australian Football League stars. Such was the hype that surrounded them.

Children

Jesinta and Buddy have two children: daughter Tullulah, born in 2020, and son Rocky, born in 2021.

Real Estate

The Franklins sold their house in Rose Bay, Sydney for a reported $4 million in 2020 and bought an apartment in the same suburb for a figure close to $5 million. They intended to retain a much smaller place in Sydney and commute for work requirements.

In December 2022, it was revealed the couple bought a seven-bedroom house on the Gold Coast. Set on a 4500sqm block that enjoys uninterrupted views over the coastline, the property was named House of the Year at the 2022 Gold Coast Master Builders Awards. Estimates put the purchase price for the property known, as "Villa Casa," at $8-10 million.

The sale was completed around the same time they put their near-new Rose Bay apartment on the market at around $5.5 million, selling it privately for around $5million to former NRL boss and head of the Australian Cricketers' Association, Todd Greenberg, and his wife Lisa.

Football

"I was fortunate to have great support from my mum and dad. Without them there is no way I would have gotten there."

Lance Franklin on his football dream

Vital stats

Age: 36 (30 Jan 2023).

Height: 199cm.

Weight: 106kg.

Chest: 119 cm.

Waist: 94 cm.

Boot size: 13 (it is reckoned 99% of his career goals have come off his left boot).

Hand span: each hand covered half a side of the Sherrin.

All-time

Fifth in all-time AFL goal scorers (1,047).

Leading goal scorer at his club 13 times (6 at Hawthorn, 7 at Sydney).

Jumper number

No. 38 first year at Hawthorn then No. 23 there and for Sydney.

Position

Key forward, mostly full-forward.

Premierships

Two – Hawthorn, 2008, 2013.

Milestones

First to reach career 1,000 goals since Gary Ablett Snr in 1996.

Most goals in a match

13, v. North Melbourne Round 10 in 2012.

Most marks in a match
13, v. St Kilda 2014.
Most kicks in a match
22, v. North Melbourne 2012.

Key career stats going into 2023
Matches played: 341
Goals scored: 1047. Behinds: 729. Goal assists: 223.
Kicks: 3649. Marks: 1859. Contested marks: 553.
Free kicks for: 440. Free kicks against: 653.
Team Win//Draw Loss records: Hawthorn – 109-1-72. Sydney – 107-0-214.
Most goals against: Essendon, 79.
Most goals at a venue: 338 MCG; 258 SCG' 172 Docklands, 100 York Stadium (Tas).
Brownlow votes: 186.
Coleman Medals: 2.
All Australian selections: 8.
Goal of the Year: 2010, 2013.

Judiciary
Guilty findings: 16; Games missed: 7. Fines total: $13,750.

Honours
AFL life membership in 2019, two premierships, eight All-Australian selections and four Coleman medals (leading goal-scorer). Sixth player to kick 1,000 goals in a career. Joined 66 other VFL/AFL players in reaching 300 career games (341 games at end of 2022 season, then 350 in June 2023).
Four times McClelland Trophy – twice Hawthorn (2012, 2013) and twice Sydney (2014, 2016) – for the best performed team in the

home-and-away competition rounds.
As at the end of the 2022 season:
AFL: 11,386th player. 25th most games played, 5th most goals kicked.
Hawthorn: 826th player. 48th most games played, 5th most goals kicked (best and fairest in 2014).
Sydney: 1,386th player. 57th most games played, 4th most goals kicked.

The early years

Franklin grew up in in Dowerin, 156 kilometres north-east of Perth in the central Wheatbelt region of Western Australia. As a youngster, he supported the Melbourne Demons Football Club in the Australian Football League.

In an interview with David King on Fox Footy program *On the Mark* in August 2019 Buddy was asked about his junior days in football. "I first rocked up, it was called back then nippers (Auskick these days) when I was about five years old. They knocked me back, said I was too small, come back the next year and I think Mum was pretty happy with that. Came back when I was six years of age and fell in love with the game of football from that day forward."

He said he began junior football as a ruckman. "I think most kids that are coming through that are pretty talented usually play in the ruck so that is what I was doing back then, just run around and have fun. Some great memories from junior age football for sure."

Buddy attended Dowerin District School from years one to 10. At the age of 15, he won a sports scholarship and boarded at Wesley College, Perth, from 2003, one of the first First Nations students to be awarded a scholarship. He earned Colours for Football in Year 11 and Honours in Year 12 after his performance in the schools'

First 18 team and gaining State representation. He also was awarded Colours for Athletics after winning the Richard Bainger Cup for Open Age Champion at the Public Schools' Association (PSA) Inter-School Athletics carnival.

During 2003 and 2004 Buddy was part of the Australian Institute of Sport (AIS)/AFL Academy. At the 2004 AFL Under 18 National Championships he represented Western Australia, kicking the winning goal in the last seconds against Victoria Metropolitan to help give his side a two-point victory.

During 2004 Buddy made his senior debut for Perth Demons (aged 17) in the West Australian Football League (WAFL).

He attended the AFL pre-draft camp for aspiring players hoping to be selected by AFL clubs. After being assessed on a variety attributes, he entered the AFL draft in November 2004 as a 17-year-old. He turned 18 on 30 January, 2005.

The 2004 Draft

Hawthorn's recruitment of Buddy Franklin almost didn't happen. The Hawks finished second last in 2004 (Richmond was bottom) and were armed with two top-five picks (three in the top-10) for the draft ahead of the 2005 season.

There were 78 picks to be drafted between 16 teams in the 2004 national draft. Richmond received the first pick. Three teams were awarded priority draft picks for winning five or fewer games: Richmond, Hawthorn and Western Bulldogs.

Hawthorn had Franklin in their sights as they developed a bold recruiting strategy, but there were two near-hiccups.

First, then-Hawks football director Dermot Brereton was involved in discussions with the West Coast Eagles which could have seen Buddy stay in Perth.

Then when it came time to nominate players in the draft, Hawthorn recruiting manager Gary Buckenara had the wrong Franklin in mind. More on that later.

Buckenara, a former Hawks player, went to Western Australia (his home state) to check on a key young key forward named Lance Franklin, playing for the state's under-18 side against an open-age group of amateur and country players. Buckenara only managed to get a brief look at Franklin's goal-kicking prowess; the teenager changed positions after the first quarter, "for the betterment of the spectacle."

Buckenara told AFL.com: "He started at centre-half forward,

but he kicked 5 goals in the first quarter and basically buggered the game for everyone else.

"They put him to centre-half-back just so he didn't destroy them completely. I thought, 'gee this kid has some talent". He was as skinny as a rake, but he was athletic, quick, tall. He was very left-sided, but he had some freakish ability.

"We continued to watch him through those years, he developed and he always stood up when he needed to stand up. He put enough runs on the board to be one of the top-10 draft picks.

"There were a few question marks back then, a lot of clubs thought he was a bit over-confident and wondered how he would go in the new AFL environment and being in the limelight.

"He was confident enough as a kid. But that's a good thing, I think. You want to see kids with belief in themselves. Buddy probably had a little bit of an extra strut or whatever in his step and in the way he handled himself, but I found him to be a really good lad," Buckenara said.

Would Hawthorn get Franklin?

Dermot Brereton met West Coast in 2004 to discuss draft picks that might secure that year's Brownlow medallist Chris Judd in exchange for the draft pick that could enable the Eagles to get Buddy Franklin.

"We knew that Chris Judd was always going to come home at some stage," Brereton told Kim Hagdorn of the *Sunday Herald Sun*. (Judd came 'home' eventually, traded to Carlton in 2007).

"I did know that we wanted to draft Buddy and, because he was a Perth boy and knowing that Judd had always intimated he would come home, I made the offer to West Coast. (I asked) whether they would be willing to swap Juddy for the draft pick that would secure Franklin."

Brereton's offer was quickly rejected and Franklin entered the draft process. Judd stayed put, winning a Norm Smith Medal, two Brownlow Medals, a premiership as captain, and multiple best and fairest awards at West Coast.

The 2004 national draft was the first for new coach Alistair Clarkson and the Hawks were keen to put that year (finishing second from the bottom) behind them and make 2005 the start of something big. They would use their top-10 draft picks judiciously.

Football manager at the time, John Hook, said Clarkson was adamant the Hawks needed to get two talls.

Buckenara had identified two talls – Franklin and Roughead – plus Geelong Falcons' Lewis who also seemed a good fit.

The Hawks thought it unlikely they could get all three, expecting the Richmond Tigers to opt for Franklin, probably with pick No. 1.

The wheeling and dealing amongst clubs for draft-pick swaps went into top gear. When the dust settled, the Hawks were aware Richmond would take Deledio at pick 1 and the Bulldogs would take Griffen at No. 3.

Richmond for some reason became less interested in Franklin as had been thought. But the Hawks knew that if they took Franklin as their first-choice tall, Richmond would most likely get Roughead at pick 4.

Instead, the Hawks surprised by taking Roughead at pick 2.

Taking Roughead was said to be a "calculated punt" to short-circuit Richmond who opted for Tambling with their No. 4 pick. That left Franklin still available – the Hawks were still in business.

Hawthorn got their man. John Hook's dealing also enabled the Hawks to get Jordan Lewis at Pick no. 7.

Hawthorn's picks set the club on a path that took it to a three-peat of premiership flags, having secured Jarryd Roughead (pick 2), Lance Franklin (pick 5) and Jordan Lewis (pick 7) in 2004.

There was debate at the time about Hawthorn taking Franklin behind other picks for Brett Deledio, who went first pick to Richmond, Jarryd Roughead (Hawthorn), Ryan Griffen (Bulldogs) and Richard Tambling (Richmond).

Buckenara said afterwards that the club had needed a strategy that would deliver Clarkson with the two key position players he was asking for.

"I thought 'how are we going to get Roughead and Franklin, the two best tall key positions', and we knew Richmond were going to take Roughead with pick four.

"Obviously they took Deledio with pick one, but we knew they'd invited Roughead to the president's welcome, so if we had taken Franklin first we wouldn't have got Roughead. So we took a punt and 'Roughie' was always going to be a really good player and a safe pick."

Buckenara said he never doubted Franklin's football abilities, but wasn't sure about his prospects of becoming an elite professional footballer. Thus, he and Hook decided to take Roughead with the second pick and hope that Franklin was still there three places later.

"Buddy had a few issues and question marks. Would he be able to cope with the AFL environment? No doubting his talent, and we sort of heard intel that Richmond had slightly gone off him, and so we took the punt and took Roughead with two", Buckenara said.

What Richmond did with its pick No. 4 was key.

"We knew Deledio would go at one, we went Roughead two, we knew the Bulldogs were taking Ryan Griffin at three, and then the question mark. So we had to wait for Richmond's pick and they went Richard Tambling and we called out Lance Franklin", Buckenara said.

"If Tambling and Lewis were still there (at pick seven), we maybe would've gone Tambling due to his pace.

"That was a pretty good start for Clarko, as those three players sort of became pillars for the side to be built around."

Franklin, Roughead and Lewis played in Hawthorn premiership teams from 2008 to 2013. Three trio also achieved All-Australian selection. Roughead retired in 2019. Lewis was traded to Melbourne in 2016 and retired in 2019.

The Buddy recruitment hiccup game as Buckenara was about to call out Franklin's name as pick No. 5 in the 2004 draft.

Gippsland teenager Luke Franklin also was in that year's draft.

Buckenara explained: "I really liked Richard Tambling as a player and he had spent a weekend at my place prior to the draft, but I did become very excited when Richmond took him at four, meaning Buddy was still available.

"In my excitement the ruler slipped down one line and I called out the number for Luke Franklin from Gippsland Power. (Coincidentally, Gippsland Power was Jarryd Roughead's original club.)

It took only 10 seconds for the mistake to be rectified, great news for Hawthorn but maybe not great news for Luke Franklin. At least he had 10 seconds of fame.

What became of Luke Franklin? He didn't get drafted, and went back to his home club at Morwell before moving to Lang Lang where he was named in its team of decade from 2001-10.

Roughead, Franklin and Lewis won 11 premierships between them, now regarded as the best first-round draft trifecta for one club in AFL history.

Lasting impressions

Geoff Slattery, managing editor *AFL Record* recalled: "I'd heard about Buddy before he was revealed in the Round One thrashing by the Sydney Swans at the SCG in 2005. At the time, Shane Crawford (Hawthorn champion player) was writing his life story and was a regular visitor to the office. I asked him about this big fella from the West. He said he was 'frightened' at how good he had been in pre-season activities. Crawford's words have resonated through the years and will continue to do so. "Franklin can do what none before him could – whether the 23s of the Hawks, or any other forward in any other era. He is the ultimate excitement machine – if only he could kick straight – at least the easy ones.

"We should never forget that in 2008, the year he became the first Indigenous centurion, he also kicked 88 behinds. In an era when forwards don't kick bags, he had 201 shots at goal. And we loved them all."

$10,000,000
OVER 9 YEARS!

In the Big League

First Nations and islander players coming from remote areas to AFL clubs face major challenges and clubs have to manage their transition carefully and Hawthorn had two First Nations leaders, Chance Bateman and Shaun Burgoyne, on their list. They helped make Buddy's transition to the Big League as comfortable as possible. In Sydney, he had Adam Goodes to admire.

"They were really people who could help kids come in at a young age and help them grow as men," Franklin once said.

"You couldn't ask for much more coming from Perth or Adelaide or remote places, you need that support. Especially if you are having troubles at home."

He was still a teenager when he took to an AFL field for the first time: Sunday 27 March 2005.

Aged 18 years and 56 days, Lance Franklin makes his AFL debut, for Hawthorn (Hawks) against Sydney (Swans) at the SCG (Sydney Cricket Ground) before a crowd of 17,274 people. He began his Hawthorn career in jumper number 38. He was the 11,368th player to appear in the VFL/AFL and the 826th player for Hawthorn.

Buddy's profile in *AFL Record Guide* to Season 2005 said: "Strong, left-footed key position player who rose to prominence in draft calculations because of his combination of size, pace, agility and sharp skills."

He recorded six disposals in his first game but failed to register a score in the clash with the eventual 2005 premiers.

He received a Rising Star nomination in Round 4 that year. He kicked 21 goals (13 behinds) in 20 games for the season. He polled only one Brownlow Medal vote (League best and fairest) that year, in Round 2 against Richmond. The Medal was won by Ben Cousins, of West Coast Eagles with 20 votes, one clear of teem-mate Daniel Kerr.

Hawthorn finished 14th in 2005, winning just five games (defeating Brisbane, Melbourne, Fremantle, Carlton, Essendon). Hawthorn was coached by Peter Schwab and Donald McDonald.

Second season – good signs

Hawthorn obviously recognised what Franklin could give the club and awarded him jumper no 23 in 2006. Several famous Hawthorn players from the more than 20 who had worn it since the club joined the League in 1925, included John Peck, Don Scott and Dermott Brereton. Alistair Clarkson took over as coach.

After injuring his ankle and hand early in the 2006 season, Buddy Franklin made his way back to senior level through the VFL, and played his first AFL game of the season in Round 9 against Sydney. In Round 12, he kicked 6 goals against Richmond. On July 13, 2006, Franklin signed a two-year deal to remain at Hawthorn after being linked with clubs such as Essendon, Fremantle and the West Coast Eagles. Another 6-goal game late in the season prompted predictions of Franklin to be the next big-name forward in the AFL. He played 14 games for the year.

Hawthorn didn't improve on its win-loss record in 2006, again winning five games. The bright spot was that four of those wins were the last four games of the season.

Franklin kicked 31 goals (9 behinds). He polled 5 Brownlow

votes for the season, 2 votes in Round 12 (against Richmond) and 3 votes in Round 19 (against Carlton).

Premiers: West Coast Eagles.

2007 – BREAKOUT YEAR

Franklin played his first full season, 22 games and was the team's leading goalkicker with 73 (62 behinds). It was a turnaround year for Franklin, and for the Hawks, winning 13 games and losing 9 to finish 5th and playing finals. They lost to North Melbourne in a semi-final after defeating Adelaide in the elimination final.

Franklin again earned 5 Brownlow Medal votes; 2 votes in Round 5 (a loss to the Western Bulldogs) and 3 votes in Round 6 (a win over Essendon).

Buddy highlight: 9 goals against Essendon in Round 6.

Premiers: Geelong Cats.

2008 – A MEDAL AND PREMIERSHIP

Hawthorn fans knew Franklin was building up to something significant in 2008. He didn't let them down with his best season since joining the Hawks. He won the Coleman Medal for the leading goal-scorer of thehome-and-away season with 102 (88 behinds). His highest "bag" for the season was 9, against Essendon again. He also played for the Dream Team in the AFL Hall of Fame Tribute Match, kicking 4 goals.

It was a stellar year for the Hawks, claiming their first AFL premiership for 17 years. They would go on to win premierships again under coach Alistair Clarkson in 2013, 2014 and 2015 - a "three-peat."

Franklin kicked his 100th goal, against Carlton in Round 22 at Etihad Stadium, becoming the first player to kick 100 goals in a season since Tony Lockett in 1998, and the first Hawthorn player since Jason Dunstall in 1996. He became the first player of First Nations descent to do so.

Playing finals saw Franklin finish the season with a goal in every one of his 25 matches. He didn't miss a game for the season, kicking 8 in the qualifying final against the Western Bulldogs, tying with Dermot Brereton for the most goals by a Hawthorn player in a final. He kicked 1 goal in the preliminary final against St Kilda and 2 goals in the Grand Final against minor premiers Geelong.

Hawthorn finished the season in second place with 17 wins, four fewer than the minor premiers who lost only one game in the home-and-away season.

Franklin's season summary: The 21-year-old's first premiership, his first Coleman Medal, his first Peter Crimmins Medal (Hawthorn Best and Fairest) and earning his first All-Australian honours. He polled 20 Brownlow medal votes, finishing just four behind medallist Adam Cooney of the Western Bulldogs, and being award three votes (best on the ground) four times. He polled votes in nine games.

Grand final: Hawthorn 115 (18.7) d Geelong 11.23 (8.9).

2009 – The hangover

Hawthorn missed the finals, becoming the first reigning premier to do so since Adelaide in 1999. The club finished ninth with just nine wins, and only made it into the top-eight five times during the season.

Franklin's season: Missed the 2009 NAB Cup (pre-season competition) after having surgery on his thumb and shoulder in the off-season. On his return to senior football, his form fell well short of his 2008 performances. He played his 100th game in Round 19 against St Kilda at Hawthorn's second home in Launceston,

Tasmania. In Round 21, Franklin was suspended for two matches (an appeal failed) after a hip-and-shoulder hit against Richmond midfielder Ben Cousins. He missed Hawthorn's final home-and-away match against Essendon, which the Hawks lost, missing the finals. His suspension put him out of Round 1 in 2010.

Franklin played 21 games, kicking 67 goals (46 behinds). His suspension ruled him out of the Brownlow medal count.

Premiers: Geelong. Brownlow Medal: Gary Ablett Jr (Geelong).

2010 – Suspensions ruin the season

Hawthorn turned their season around somewhat in 2010, making it to seventh on the ladder and playing finals again.

Franklin missed three of the first seven matches of 2010, all through suspension, and was suspended in Round 10 for a third time in eight matches for a head-high bump on Sydney Swans' defender Martin Mattner.

Hawthorn lost six matches in a row after Round 1. Franklin had returned to form in Round 9, helping the Hawks triumph over Carlton with 5 goals. His career average to that point was more than 3 goals a game (324 goals in 106 games after Round 9).

In Round 13, Franklin effectively got Hawthorn over the line against Essendon, kicking 5 goals for the match, his last one from the boundary line on a tight angle after having run from half-back. That goal was later chosen as goal-of-the year.

Franklin kicked 5 goals in the Round 17 draw against St Kilda after returning from an ankle injury, and in Round 22, he kicked 6 goals against Collingwood for a three-point come-from-behind victory against the eventual premiers. It was the first time that he had kicked more than 5 goals since 2008. Franklin was again named in the All-Australian team that year. Suspensions ruled him out of

Brownlow Medal contention. He played 18 games, kicking 64 goals (42 behinds).

Hawthorn lost to Frementle in the elimination finals. Collingwood and St Kilda drew the Grand Final, Collingwood going on to win the replay a week later.

Premiers: Collingwood. Brownlow: Chris Judd (Carlton).

2011 – Another Coleman Medal

Hawthorn continued to improve, finishing third on the ladder after winning 18 of 22 matches in the home-and-away season. The Hawks lost the qualifying final to Geelong, then defeated Sydney comfortably in the semi-final before losing narrowly to minor premiers Collingwood in the preliminary final.

Franklin's season: In Round 8 against the Sydney Swans at the SCG, Franklin kicked his 400th goal for Hawthorn in a 6-goal effort in a 46-point victory. He kicked a season-high 8 goals in a club-record 165-point win against Port Adelaide side at the MCG in Round 21. His 71 goals for the season earned him a second Coleman Medal. He appeared to suffer a serious knee injury in the qualifying loss to Geelong, but recovered to play the next game, kicking 4 goals in the win over the Swans. A virus put him in hospital in the lead-up to the preliminary final yet he managed 3 goals. He was named at full-forward in the All-Australian team for the second time. Suspension again ruled Franklin out of Brownlow Medal contention.

Premiers: Geelong. Brownlow Medal: Dane Swan (Collingwood).

2012 – Milestone and disappointment

Hawthorn came within a whisker of taking the premiership, going down by just 10 points to the Sydney Swans in the Grand Final at the MCG.

It was a mixed season for Buddy Franklin; he kicked a career high for a match – 13 goals in a 115-points thrashing of North Melbourne, then having to miss several weeks with a hamstring injury, playing only 19 matches for the season (including the finals).

He began the season shakily, kicking 21 goals and 36 behinds in his first nine matches. He became one of five players that year to reach the milestone of 500 career goals, in a 162-point thrashing League of newcomers Greater Western Sydney in Round 15. He became the second First Nations player to reach 500 goals, the fifth Hawthorn player, the seventh-youngest and the tenth-quickest from debut. He suffered a hamstring injury the previous week but continued to play, before injuring it further in the Giants game, the injury and illness causing him to miss six matches. He returned against the Sydney Swans at the SCG in Round 22, kicking 4 goals in a seven-point come-from-behind win over the eventual premiers. He didn't have much impact in the finals, but kicked a goal late in the last quarter of the preliminary final against the Adelaide Crows to seal a Grand Final place for the Hawks. He kicked 3 goals in the losing Grand Final side. He was named in the 2012 All-Australian team, his fourth selection and second as centre-half-forward.

Buddy kicked 69 goals (64 behinds) in the home-and-away season and polled 12 Brownlow Medal votes – 3 votes three times and 1 vote three times.

Premiers: Sydney Swans. Brownlow medal: Jobe Watson (Essendon).

2013 – Another premiership

This was the last year of Franklin's latest (four-year) contract with the Hawks, and 10th overall. He was classified as a restricted free agent, meaning Hawthorn could retain him with an acceptable offer. Greater Western Sydney (GWS) loomed as a possible suitor. He kicked 60 goals (37 behinds) in the season, the first time since 2006 that he averaged less than 3 a game. Teammate Jarryd Roughead was the club's leading goal-scorer with 72. A shot in Round 3 earned Franklin his second Goal of the Year. The Hawks finished minor premiers with 19 wins. Franklin polled 5 Brownlow votes, 1 vote twice and 3 votes once.

Hawthorn defeated Fremantle in the Grand Final, Franklin kicking just 1 goal in his second premiership year with the Hawks.

Franklin travelled to Ireland with the Australian International Rules team for the 2013 International Rules Series. It was the first time that Franklin had represented Australia in international rules football.

Grand Final: Hawthorn 77 (11.11) defeated Fremantle 62 (8.14).

Brownlow Medal: Gary Ablett Jr (Gold Coast).

Swan Song

The 2013 season drama didn't finish with Grand Final glory. Franklin's contract negotiations continued: GWS withdrew its offer of $1.2 million a year for six years. Sydney weighed in with a nine-year deal worth $10 million. Hawthorn didn't match it. Franklin officially joined the Sydney Swans on 8 October. John Longmire was in his fourth year as coach.

2014 – Sydney Swans debut

Keeping his No. 23 jumper number, now in red and white, Franklin played his first game for the Swans on Saturday 30 March in the Round 1 Sydney Derby against cross-town rivals GWS at Spotless Stadium, kicking just 1 goal for the game in an upset loss.

Four weeks later against North Melbourne, Buddy was then held goalless for the only time that season. He returned to form against Fremantle at the SCG, kicking 4 second-half goals. In round 8 he faced his old club Hawthorn and kicked 2 fourth-quarter goals to help the Swans to an upset victory. He went on to win his third Coleman Medal, kicking 67 goals in 19 matches. He posted a career-high Brownlow Medal tally of 22 votes, finishing joint second with Gary Ablett Jr and behind Matt Priddis (West Coast) on 26.

Sydney reached the Grand Final, losing to the Hawks 134 (21.11) to 74 (11.8).

Franklin kicked 4 goals (2 behinds) in the 2014 AFL Grand Final loss to Sydney, his highest tally in a Grand Final. He played all three finals matches.

Franklin also played his 200th game during the season, kicking a season-high 9 goals in Round 19 against St Kilda at the SCG.

2015 – Injury and illness

Franklin began the 2015 season with a 3-goal performance against Essendon. His form held up through the season, including 7 goals against Carlton at the SCG in Round 9.

He finished the year with 47 goals (29 behinds) from 17 games, missing four of the last seven games due to a back injury. It was the first time since 2006 that he kicked fewer than 50 goals or played fewer than 18 games in a season. He withdrew from playing in the finals series due to a mental illness.

He polled 8 Brownlow votes for the year, 3 votes twice and 2 votes once. He posted his 700th career goal in Round 16.

Sydney finished fourth on the ladder with 16 wins, the same number as Hawthorn and West Coast who went on to play the Grand Final. Sydney bowed out losing to Fremantle (minor premiers) and North Melbourne.

Premiers: Hawthorn. Brownlow Medal: Nat Fyfe (Fremantle).

2016 – Back on target

Franklin had his eye in, kicking 4 goals in each of the first four rounds, following up with 2 against the Eagles, 5 against the Lions and 6 against the Bombers. He kicked 81 for the season (54 behinds) in his best season for several years, playing all 26 games. He polled 17 Brownlow votes in 10 games including two 3-vote games and was runner up in the Coleman Medal.

It was almost an excellent year for the Swans, too, winning 19 games and finishing as minor premiers with 17 wins along with Western Bulldogs and Hawthorn. The Swans went on to play in the Grand Final, the Western Bulldogs winning 89 (13.11) to 67 (10.7), after finishng 7th on the League ladder.

It wasn't a good year for some players; 34 of them missed the season through suspension by the World Anti-Doping Agency, for doping infringements which occurred at the Essendon Football Club as part of its 2012 sports supplements program.

Brownlow Medal: Patrick Dangerfield (Geelong).

2017 – Kicking goals again

Franklin returned to football after off-season shoulder surgery in a practice match against GWS in March where he showed no ill-affects, kicking the first two goals.

He had quite a year. As well as being selected as an All-Australian key forward for the seventh time, and winning his fourth Coleman Medal as leading goalkicker with 73 (60 behinds), he was voted an AFL Players Association's MVP of the month for the first time. He kicked 18 goals in the last four home-and-away rounds.

He polled 22 Brownlow votes, one behind teammate Josh Kennedy. He played his 250th game in Round 3. He kicked his 800th goal in Round 5. He played 24 games including finals.

Sydney became the first club to reach the finals after starting the season with six straight losses, eventually scrambling into the top-eight at sixth position. Adelaide, Geelong and Richmond each had 15 wins, GWS, Port Adelaide and Sydney each had 14. Adelaide's record of 15 wins, 1 draw and 6 losses was the least successful of any minor premier since 1997.

Premiers: Richmond. Brownlow Medal: Dustin Martin (Richmond).

2018 – A mixed bag

Franklin suffered some injury setbacks but capped off the year by being named All-Australian team captain.

It was his fifth All-Australian selection at centre half-forward, third in succession and record-equalling eighth overall.

He began the season with his largest opening-round haul of 8 goals against West Coast in Perth.

There was a cost; he missed the next three weeks after sustaining a bruised heel. He kicked 3 goals in Round 9 against Fremantle at the SCG, including his 300th goal as a Swan, becoming only the second player after Tony Lockett to kick 300 goals for two clubs. Coach Longmire revealed Franklin had not been able to do much serious training due to heel injuries. He missed the last home-and-away game with a groin injury.

In Round 15, he played his 100th game for Sydney, kicking 4 goals in the loss to Richmond.

Two weeks later, he kicked his 900th career goal with the first of his 3 goals in a 6-point win over North Melbourne. He was kept goalless in the elimination final loss to GWS, only the second time he failed to score for the season. Sydney finished 6th in the home-and-away series with 14 wins.

Franklin played 19 games for the year, kicking 57 goals (43 behinds) and polling 16 Brownlow Medal votes (four 3-votes, a 2 and one 1). He had surgery on his groin and was unable to train at the end of the season. He also had a hip injury during the season.

Premiers: West Coast. Brownlow Medal: Tom Mitchell (Hawthorn).

2019 – Beset by injury

Franklin began the season with concerns about his fitness after undergoing groin surgery in the off-season and not having a full pre-season. He missed 12 games through injury, mostly hamstring-related, playing only 10. He hadn't played since round 14 in June before returning for his 300th on 24 August, at home against St Kilda in round 22, and kicking 4 goals. He was among the best on the field in that game, taking 10 marks.

Franklin managed 27 goals (18 behinds) for the season. He polled 3 Brownlow Medal votes from two matches. The Swans had a disappointing season, finishing 15th with just eight wins. It was Sydney's first absence from the finals series since Franklin joined the club.

For only the second time, neither of the top two teams after the home-and-away series (Geelong and Brisbane) reached the Grand Final and GWS played in their first grand final.

Premiers: Richmond. Brownlow Medal: Nat Fyfe (Fremantle).

The lost year

2020 – Was this the end?

The year was a disaster for all involved with football, no matter how it was analysed and particularly so for Buddy Franklin.

In January, Franklin underwent an arthroscope on his right knee; the club thought he would resume full training in 10 weeks, missing the Round 1 match against Adelaide.

As things turned out, that was the only round played before the 2020 season was suspended because of the Covid-19 pandemic that gripped Australia and the world.

Franklin was on track to return for the resumption of the season in June until he suffered a hamstring injury in late May.

At the start of the year, Franklin was added to a Swans leadership group for the first time in his career.

The season resumed on 11 June and ran until 24 October, played under Covid-safe protocols and comprising a 17-game home-and-away series followed by the finals. All matches were shortened to 80% of their usual length. Virus outbreaks and interstate travel restrictions precluded games in some states, with all clubs spending parts of the season temporarily relocated to quarantine hubs, particularly in South East Queensland where almost half of all matches were played, including the Grand Final, the first time it had been played outside Victoria. Health directives resulted in restricted match attendances throughout the year and 30 matches were played behind closed doors.

In August, Franklin was ruled out for the rest of the season after developing groin soreness during his rehabilitation.

Many pundits predicted Buddy Franklin was at the end of his career when he had to sit out the 2020 season and the first week of 2021.

His injury record wasn't good. He'd last played a full season in 2017 and had played just 10 games in 2019 and only one since June that year. He'd suffered two hamstring injuries, both to his left leg.

He had knee surgery in January 2020 and was to miss the start of the season, his seventh with the Sydney Swans since leaving Hawthorn on a mega nine-year deal.

As the 2020 season approached, he was looking to step up his training for what he hoped would be a successful return to the field towards the end of the season. But he was stung by another injury, this time to his hamstring on his right side, the same side as his injured knee which required surgery in January.

A report by Lauren N. Erickson and Marc A. Sherry in the *Journal of Sport and Health Science* (US), notes hamstring strain injuries are "common among sports that involve sprinting, kicking, and high-speed skilled movements or extensive muscle lengthening-type manoeuvres with hip flexion and knee extension."

A serious hamstring injury definitely was not what a big mobile goal-kicking forward needed on top of everything else.

"It's been a frustrating three years with injuries," Franklin said. "With my groins, both knees, heel, there's been a number of injuries.

"That happens, injuries happen in football. There's not much we can do about it."

Of course an extra strain on everyone, footballers not excluded, were the Covid-19 restrictions imposed on all facets of life over 2020-2021. They impacted severely on AFL players and their families with games moved away from Victoria where lockdown rules were harshest.

Former Hawthorn star Dermot Brereton had said the Hawks thought Franklin would only make it to 2020 when he left to join the Sydney Swans. The hamstring injury in May made that look a real possibility.

But then-Hawthorn coach Alistair Clarkson didn't go along with that school of thought. "I wouldn't write him off by any means," Clarkson said.

At that point, the four-time Coleman medallist was in the seventh season of a huge nine-year, $10 million deal.

Could he see out his contract by playing on to the end of 2022 and even beyond?

It wouldn't have surprised Clarkson that Buddy recovered from that setback and did play on beyond his initial contract.

"(Franklin's) had the best part of 12 months now where it's been tough for him but I know him very well as a person," Clarkson said.

"He's made fantastic contributions to both the Hawthorn and Sydney footy clubs. He's a long way from finishing up.

"He's been such a durable bugger for a long, long period of time at both of our clubs.

"He'll be doing it tough at the minute but he'll find a way and play some footy again."

At the time of his hamstring injury in 2020, he was 34 years old. He'd kicked 944 goals. He had played in two premierships (with Hawthorn) and few would have been terribly surprised if he'd "pulled the pin" then.

He pulled up sore at the end of a training session before the season started. Scans confirmed he avoided tendon damage, but would be facing a long stint out of the game.

Sydney head of football Charlie Gardiner said it was "slightly worse" than the left hamstring injury Franklin suffered the previous year when he missed nine weeks. It turned out this time that it was quite a severe injury and he would miss the whole year.

Wife Jesinta told how devastated Buddy was after suffering the injury in a running drill at training.

"It's absolutely devastating," she told Channel Seven.

"He came home yesterday from training early and he was really upset by what had happened.

"He'd spent the whole pre-season working so hard, even in lockdown, he'd focused so much on staying fit and healthy which is really hard when you're not training with your teammates and there's no fixture in sight and no idea when you're going back to play.

"It's really unfortunate, I think it's just part and parcel in playing professional sport and it's what happens and you've just got to keep positive," she said.

He was tough and even after 17 years of football he still had the passion to be playing.

No. Buddy wasn't giving up.

The spur to continue may have been joining the elite group of players who had kicked 1,000 career goals. He'd be among some of the game's greats if he did: Tony Lockett (1,360), Gordon Coventry (1,299), Jason Dunstall (1,254), Doug Wade (1,057) and Gary Ablett Sr (1,031). Buddy was still 56 goals short.

According to the Erickson/Sherry report, hamstring injuries involved a challenge of significant recovery time and a lengthy period of increased susceptibility for recurrent injury.

"Nearly one third of hamstring strains recur within the first year following return to sport with subsequent injuries often being more severe than the original, the NML says. "This high re-injury rate suggests that athletes may be returning to sport prematurely due to inadequate return to sport criteria."

Buddy made a tentative return to the playing field on Sunday 21 March in 2021, by way of a 60-minutes appearance for the Swans against the Giants in a reserves scratch match.

There was special news that week – Buddy and Jesinta announced the birth of their second child, Rocky, a brother for Tullulah, who was born in February 2020. Both were highlights in what were a couple of terrible years football-wise.

2021– The comeback

Franklin bounced back in 2021, kicking 51 goals in his 18-game season despite suffering a number of calf and knee setbacks. He suffered calf soreness leading into the 2021 season and missed the Round 1 victory against the Brisbane Lions.

The football season heavily impacted by the Covid pandemic as matches were played under lockdown rules, without crowds and many teams having to travel away from home into hubs.

The League's Grand Finals had to be shifted from the Melbourne Cricket Ground traditional venue again, to Optus Stadium in Perth after being moved to the 'Gabba, Brisbane, in 2020

Buddy said in an interview: "The 2021 season for the AFL, like any industry, definitely came with its challenges. It wasn't easy being relocated away from my family. I was fortunate to have the support from my wife Jesinta, who ended up joining the hub allowing us to be together as a family with our young children."

Buddy played 18 games, kicking 51 goals (24 behinds) and polling 8 Brownlow Medal votes, including 3 votes once.

It was a case of "what might have been" for the Swans, going down by just one point to cross-town rivals GWS in the elimination final after finishing sixth in the home-and-away season.

Premiers: Melbourne (first for 57 years). Brownlow Medal: Ollie Wines (Port Adelaide).

2022 – A Milestone

Everyone was fairly confident Buddy Franklin would reach 1,000 goals during the 2022 season. He did so with a 4-goal haul on 26 March in Sydney in a 30-point win over Geelong.

Sydney went all the way to the Grand Final, losing to Geelong in what was a major let-down for the club. Franklin played 23 games for the season.

He scored 52 goals (28 behinds) for the season and polled 8 Brownlow votes, a 3, two 2s and a 1.

Sydney was inside the top eight all season and finished third on the ladder, behind Geelong (minor premiers) and Melbourne. The Swans defeated Melbourne and Collingwood (by a point) on their way to the Grand Final before crashing to a 71-point loss to Geelong. Franklin didn't kick a goal in the Grand Final. It was a lean finals series for Franklin; he didn't score in the qualifying final win over Melbourne, but he kicked two important goals in the preliminary final against Collingwood.

The season was played under a hangover from the Covid restrictions of the two previous years.

The league implemented a Vaccination Policy requiring all players and football department staff to be vaccinated against COVID-19. Two players – Liam Jones (Carlton) and Cam Ellis-Yolmen (Brisbane Lions) – retired as a result of the mandate. The AFL mandate ended in July, about the same times as State Government orders ended.

A player top-up list and policy was brought in to cover for a large number of players having to go into isolation. Each club could nominate 20 top-up players from their affiliated state league and reserves systems; they would be eligible to play if fewer than 28 main list players were available due to Covid reasons. The West Coast Eagles whose home state had tighter restrictions than others, was the only club to draw on its top-up list, doing so twice.

At the end of the season, the main talking point was whether Buddy Franklin would play on. His contract with Sydney was done and he would be 36 years old in January. Would he stay with Sydney or move on to finish his career somewhere else?

He wasn't the oldest AFL player of the modern era - Dustin Fletcher of Essendon finished his career aged 40, albeit only the second to be still playing at that age (the other was Melbourne's Vic Cumberland in 1900).

And if Buddy did play on beyond 2022, could he make it through an entire season, given his injury woes of recent years?

How the Swans swooped

A harsh reality of Buddy Franklin's switch to the Sydney Swans from the Hawthorn Hawks in 2014 is that the Hawks went on to win two more premierships without him and the Swans hadn't won any with him.

He was going to move on from the Hawks, and Sydney eventually was his chosen destination, "to win more premierships." Franklin was at Hawthorn for nine seasons after he was drafted in 2004.

In 2013 he was in the final year of his latest four-year contract with the Hawks. When his contract expired at the end of 2013, he was entitled either to get a renewal or move on as a "restricted free agent."

Out-of-contract players within the top 25% paid players at their club become restricted free agents after eight seasons, then become unrestricted free agents after ten seasons.

Hawthorn could retain Franklin if they matched offers put to him by another club. He was hot property, and any number of clubs would want him on their playing roster.

Franklin in February 2013 ruled out any contract talks with Hawthorn until the end of the season, sparking talk he would be making a move.

The two Sydney clubs certainly were interested, the fledgling Greater Western Sydney (GWS) appearing to be the frontrunner to secure his signature as speculation on the star's future kicked into overdrive at the start of the season.

There were a number of reasons a move was on the cards. First, Franklin was keen to move closer to his new girlfriend (and future wife). When it came to choosing between the two Sydney teams, he most likely saw the Swans as having better premiership credentials than the Giants. And there was the Adam Goodes factor. From the Swans' point of view, having the League's best goal-scorer on their books increased the possibility of more premiership glory.

Franklin also had the star quality that would increase Sydney's profile among the local population. As Marc McGowan noted on afl.com.au, "Sydney's membership base spiked from about 36,000 pre-Buddy to beyond 60,000, while home crowds, corporate sponsorship, merchandise sales and Swans matches in marquee timeslots all went up."

There was no doubt Hawthorn wanted to keep Franklin but at what cost? The Hawks were prepared to go to a five-year contract renewal worth about $5 million. But could they afford to lose such an asset if that wasn't enough?

The Hawks had to weight up the amount of their salary-cap (estimated at $1.1-$1.3 million) that was tied up with Buddy compared to what they could do if he left.

The Hawks did have options to fill the void up forward. Jack Gunston had kicked 11.4 in three finals appearances. They also had Bruest (their leading goal-scorer in the 2013 Grand Final victory) and Roughead, both capable goal-scoring options. (Hawthorn went on to finish a three-peat of premierships after winning with Buddy in 2013 then without him in 2014 and 2015).

On 1 October 2013, after months of speculation, GWS revealed it had withdrawn its offer of $1.2 million per year for six years, believing Franklin had committed to the Swans. They were right.

Franklin's manager at the time was Liam Pickering. Pickering managed Franklin's move from Hawthorn to the Sydney Swans at the end of 2013, securing a lucrative a nine-year contract.

The Swans swooped, paying $10 million over nine years to blow the Hawks out of the water, GWS also out of the bidding by then. The Swans got a player fresh off a premiership-winning season.

While Sydney saw that Franklin's goalkicking prowess could deliver them premierships, they also knew a nine-year deal for "megabucks" was something of a risk.

Swans chief executive Andrew Ireland acknowledged as much.

"We're confident it's a very fair deal for Lance... if he plays the way he can it will be a very good deal for Sydney," he said.

Coach John Longmire and the Swans players were pleased to have Franklin in the squad.

"I guess the general feeling is if he's up here to work hard, train hard and make us better... then great," Longmire said.

"It's pretty simple if you work hard and you train hard and you play well on the weekend that's all we ask for...

"We want to be at the top part of the ladder for a number of years, and we feel Lance can help us do that."

As for Franklin, he said he had no doubts he could see out the contract. Asked at a press conference if he saw himself still playing in nine seasons time, he replied: "definitely," adding "I love playing my football. I love getting out there. I love training. I can definitely see myself playing until I'm that age.

"I think there's a lot of good football left in me. As long as I'm having a good pre-season and doing everything right, I'm going to be playing good football."

Why not GWS? According to the pundits and commentators, Buddy was all-but signed to GWS until the Swans swooped.

"In the end of the day, I wanted to come to a club that was going to win more premierships," Franklin said at the time.

"GWS are going to be great, no doubt, but that's probably four to five years (away), I want success pretty much straight away, that's why I chose Sydney."

Franklin parted ways with manager Pickering mid-way through his first Sydney season, in June 2014. It was a curious move with little by way of explanation being offered publicly.

The move came as a shock to Pickering who said he'd been travelling to Sydney once a week in 2014 to help Franklin get organised as he settled into a new city

"He thought he needed someone in Sydney, and that is disappointing but it's life. I don't have any problems with Bud, I love Bud ... I want him to do well for the year, but I was a bit shocked at the time I must say," Pickering said.

Franklin moved to a celebrity management company with no other AFL footballers as clients at the time.

"From a football perspective, I think a sounding board that has got a football background is ideal for Buddy," Pickering told AFL.com's Peter Ryan.

Buddy and wife Jesinta initially were managed by Annie Kelly from The Agency Inc. In 2022, football inquiries were directed to Adam Finch, who had become Jesinta's full-time manager and then handled Franklin and his football interests.

Finch, a former teacher, had been the business manager of Buddy Promotions and Jesinta Franklin Enterprises for a year. Pickering had been Franklin's manager since he joined Hawthorn.

"I'm actually not filthy at all. I understand people can get in his ear," Pickering said. "His main job is football."

Franklin's eagerness for immediate success with Sydney, in terms of premierships, didn't go all that well. After nine years, there was still nothing more in the trophy cabinet. Sydney's last premiership was in 2012. That didn't mean securing Franklin had been a failure, far from it.

In Buddy's first year, the Swans became the first non-South Australian team to win at Adelaide Oval defeating Adelaide by 63 points with Franklin and Luke Parker kicking 4 goals each.

The Swans also defeated the Grand Finalists from the previous year (Hawthorn and Fremantle) and won a dozen games in a row to secure their first minor premiership in 18 years and unsuccessfully contest the Grand Final, Franklin becoming one of just a few players to play in successive Grand Finals for different teams.

During Buddy's nine-year deal, the Swans appeared in three Grand Finals, losing to Hawthorn in 2014, the Western Bulldogs in 2016 and Geelong in 2022.

Franklin's best year was 2018 when he kicked 57 goals in 19 matches. In 2021 season, when he had a team-best 51 goals in 18 matches. He was always a crowd favourite in home games.

Whether Franklin could have helped GWS to a maiden premiership is unknown.

Franklin had also said one of the motivating factors in moving to Sydney was the ability to play with dual Brownlow Medallist Adam Goodes.

"I'm excited and pumped to get out there this year and play with the likes of Adam Goodes, I remember lining up here in round one, debut season and him coming to me and playing on me," he said. "Now I get the chance to play alongside Goodsey, it's something I'm looking forward to and can't wait to get out there."

The former Hawthorn superstar said the decision to leave was one of the hardest he had ever made.

"Only I know how it felt (to leave)," he said. "I love the Hawthorn football club to death still.

"I won two premierships with Hawthorn and I walk away from Hawthorn football club very proud of what I achieved."

He said when he had told Hawks coach Alastair Clarkson of his move the coach was surprised but still shook his hand and wished him well.

"I couldn't speak highly enough of Clarko and the Hawthorn football club and the boys that I've played football with," Franklin said.

There's no mistake losing Franklin was a major loss. But it did have a financial silver lining; the Hawks saved a million dollars a year in their salary cap, allowing them to retain almost every player on their "keep" list through 2013.

Hawthorn won three successive premierships; 2013 (Franklin's last year for 1 goal in the Grand Final), 2014 and 2015. Sydney had won the premiership in 2012, defeating the Hawthorn side that included Franklin who kicked 3 goals and was rated among the losing side's better players on the day.

Before sanctioning the move to Sydney, the AFL sought written guarantees the contract payment would be made in full, regardless of how long Franklin played, and would count against Sydney's salary cap. This reflected concerns about whether Buddy could go another nine seasons.

The deal went through.

Franklin again was the subject of much transfer speculation during 2022, with his nine-year Swans deal due to expire.

The talk was that he'd go to Brisbane.

Swans CEO Tom Harley said reports Franklin wanted to move to the Brisbane Lions, was "news to me."

"There's no hurry (about contract talks) from our point of view and no hurry from his point of view," Harley said.

"Things are all tracking well."

In the end, Franklin opted for a 10th season at the Swans.

The 2022 Grand Final loss to Geelong was a game the Swans – and Buddy – would hope to forget quickly.

Extending his stay would give the now famous No. 23 a chance to overtake Doug Wade in the list of AFL's greatest goalkickers, needing 11 to do that.

More importantly for Buddy the 2023 season would be a chance to redeem himself after barely troubling the statisticians in the Grand Final; he had only five possessions for the game, kicking just a single point when he hit the post from close range early in the second quarter. He wasn't alone among the Swans players who didn't perform to expectations in the 81-point trashing by Geelong.

His old club Hawthorn found the going tough on several fronts. The club hasn't appeared in the AFL finals since 2018. Coach Alistair Clarkson stepped down in 2021 (replaced by former player Sam Mitchell and finished 13th on the ladder). The club was rocked by racism allegations and a sometimes-bitter boardroom election battle in 2022.

FOOTNOTE:

The Sydney Swans' origins go back to 21 March 1873, when a junior football club, to be called the South Melbourne Football Club, was established. The club first played in 1874 at its home ground, Lakeside Oval in Albert Park, close to the suburb of South Melbourne. South Melbourne was in the Victorian Football Association (VFA) competition from 1878 before joining the breakaway Victorian Football League (VFL) as a founding member in 1897. Originally known as the "Bloods" (they wore red jumpers), the Swan emblem was adopted in 1933, a year in which they won the premiership. It was a long wait until their next premiership success – 72 years, in 2005.

In 1980 and 1981, the team played two matches at the SCG to see if Sydney would accept an AFL team, being a city where the rugby codes were strongest. Souths were interested in making a move, the club having found itself facing financial issues. Moving home games to Sydney was seen as a solution.

But things got ugly from July 1981 into 1982 before the move eventually was sanctioned. There were legal challenges, player meetings, strike threats over payments, board and coaching upheavals before peace was restored.

The Club maintained its Victorian base with players flying to Sydney for their 11 home games in 1982.

A year later the club adopted the name, Sydney Swans with the SCG as its new home ground.

The South Melbourne Swans became the first Australian football club to permanently relocate interstate, overcoming a strong campaign from a "Keep Souths at Souths" movement.

BEHIND EVERY SUCCESSFUL MAN...

The lives of Jesinta and Buddy Franklin have fascinated Australian magazines and gossip columns ever since their first date.

They've been a rich vein of gold for the glossy mags, even the "tabloid" columnists – romance between a beauty pageant queen and one of the brightest Australian Football League stars.

All grist for the magazines mill.

Vogue, Women's Day, New Idea, Who, Marie Claire all saw the mileage in anything to do with the world of modelling, glamour romance and beauty that their readers crave.

Websites such as NowtoLove and Mamamia didn't miss out either. That's not to say everything that's been published about them has been accurate. There's always been gossip and it was rampant during Buddy's sabbatical from football to deal with mental health issues.

Jesinta had a message for journalists and commentators: stick to "things that actually have weight to them."

Mostly the publicity hype has been about Jesinta through her media profile. Buddy remains a generally private person.

As a beauty pageant contestant, Jesinta enjoyed success: a Miss Universe Australia title in 2010 and representing Australia in that year's Miss Universe pageant where she was second runner-up and won the Miss Congeniality award.

She was Jesinta Campbell in those times, born and raised on the

Gold Coast, itself a home of glamour and hype.

The story got better when she matched up with the footballing hunk Lance "Buddy" Franklin.

Jesinta and Buddy first met in 2013 when they were both in their early 20s.

Jesinta recalled that at first, she rejected Buddy's advances.

"He got my number from someone (a mutual friend) , and then he just started messaging me. And I was like, 'Um, I'm not dating at the moment. I'm dating my career,'" she told *Beauticate.com* in 2017.

"Cringe! Oh my God, I can't believe I said that. Back then, as soon as I came back from competing at Miss Universe, I hit the ground and the years following were insanely busy. Weekends were non-existent, and I never took any holidays. I was so busy I couldn't imagine fitting in any dating."

A few months later they went on their first date.

They became engaged in December 2014 and married in a private ceremony attended by their immediate families and close friends in a garden in the Blue Mountains, NSW, in November 2016.

Jesinta has had television roles and published a book, *Live a Beautiful Life*, in October 2016.

When Buddy launched a clothing line, Buddy Franklin Authentic, in 2018, Jesinta was heavily involved.

"I'm kind of like doing all the back end of that... the accounts, the finances, the ordering," she said.

"He likes to call himself the CEO, who just comes in and oversees everything. He's even got a business card that says CEO on it."

They've kept their lives as private as possible since. Buddy concentrates on his football career and Jesinta remains active in social media, influencing, promotion and speaking out on significant issues. In 2022 she signed up as model for Seafolly swimwear.

Jesinta said in one interview that she and Buddy encouraged each other in their ambitions.

They've been subject to public scrutiny, dealt with miscarriages and endured long periods apart (including football Covid hubs that separated them for nearly two years) to evolve into a comfortable family unit.

The couple are raising their two children, daughter Tullulah and son Rocky, both born over 12 months, February 2020 to March 2021. The football media almost went into meltdown in July 2022 when it was revealed Jesinta had taken an active interest in football administration.

"Jesinta Franklin is making a bizarre career hop that nobody saw coming in a move that could get awkward for her husband," shouted a news report on 7 July 2022.

The report went on: "Jesinta Franklin is about to become an accredited player agent with the AFL. It was revealed... the 30-year-old fashion and lifestyle influencer has completed the AFL Players' Association's accreditation course in an application for official AFLPA registration.

"The AFLPA has confirmed it is assessing recent applications.

"The former Miss Universe Australia turned businesswoman would be able to represent her husband, Sydney Swans star Lance Franklin, in ongoing contract negotiations if her papers are rubber stamped."

She did the course, but her name did not appear on the register of accredited agents for 2022-23. She didn't become Buddy's player-manager.

She later told the *Herald-Sun*'s Fiona Byrne: "I am accredited but I haven't done anything with that at the moment. I probably won't do anything until the kids get to school, but I did my accreditation to learn a bit more about the industry and broaden my understanding, and get to know the landscape a little bit.

"There are definitely future plans with that, but nothing in the immediate future."

FranklinFinch Management Pty Ltd was registered in September 2022; the directors are Jesinta Franklin and Adam Finch, a former teacher who became the business manager of Buddy Promotions and Jesinta Franklin Enterprises. According to *au.companiesdb.net*, the location of the private company is Griffith NSW.

Jesinta still has an on-line profile, including an app that allows her to contact her followers on a more personal level.

Jesinta has played a significant role in Buddy's football life anyway, particularly in times when he had injury and health issues.

Buddy credited her with her helping him get through those difficult times.

He acknowledged his support network for helping get through his mental health issues that surfaced in 2015, particularly his then fiancée Jesinta (Campbell).

"I've got such a great support network around me in my partner and family and friends, the football club have been terrific in this tough time and I couldn't be more thankful," he said.

Buddy and Jesinta postponed their wedding that was scheduled for January 2016 to focus on his health.

Jesinta has featured in magazine articles talking about the issues that affect and concern her, hoping to increase awareness in the community of the difficulties some people face.

"I know from firsthand experiences and seeing people close to me go through it, how much courage that takes," she said in one interview. She hoped that talking about her experience with a close family member and Buddy would help break down the stigma associated with mental illness.

She told *Marie Claire* magazine she lost an aunt to suicide. "I can't even put into words the feeling when I got the phone call – and even now it doesn't seem real. It still is an awful time for our whole family," she said.

"[My aunt] was someone I was close to, someone the whole family knew struggled. But the hard pill for all of us to swallow is that we never had that really deep conversation with her. So [if] I can talk more about [mental health issues], hopefully [it will compel] a person who knows someone going through it to have a conversation with that person, or if they're going through it themselves, they'll feel compelled to have a conversation with someone they trust, and that saves a life."

She revealed she sought professional help herself to "download all my worries and stresses."

"I don't have any fear of talking about it and being open about my mental health or helping those around me feel more comfortable talking about it."

There seems little doubt that Jesinta was a key driver of Buddy's decision to keep going in football at the end of his nine-year deal with Sydney.

She supported him amid the rumours that were flying around about him during contract machinations in 2022, acknowledging her husband had options beyond his last contract year with the Swans.

"There's always rumours and speculation swirling around Bud, and I think when he's coming to the end of such an amazing contract, this was always going to happen," she told Channel 7.

"But I think they're just that; they're rumours and they're speculation.

"I still feel like he's got lots to give, and he still feels like he's got great footy (left in him), and he feels so good.

"He keeps saying, 'I feel like I'm 21,' which is great. And the stats really show that as well."

She had said she could see her family moving interstate to be closer to family sometime.

"I think there's still a lot of good football left in him, but it's our dream, whether that's in five years or 10 years or whenever, to be able to live closer to one of the grandparents and have quality time with them," she said.

The story-hungry media went into overdrive later in 2022 when the couple forked out about $9 million on a glamorous Mediterranean-style mansion on the Gold Coast, weeks before listing their luxury apartment in Sydney's Eastern Suburbs for sale.

Many surmised Buddy would be going north for one more year of elite level football, but he'd already decided to stay with the Swans, commuting from the Gold Coast if he had to.

Jesinta remained keen to keep their children out of the limelight as much as possible as they grow up with First Nations heritage.

Jesinta told a magazine: "I've never been judged for the colour of my skin, my culture, where I was born or who my parents are. It's not my lived experience, but it is Buddy's and his mum's and sisters'.

"Obviously, I'm guided by Buddy, but I've also taken the initiative to educate myself so I can be the best mum to our First Nations babies and the best ally I can be. I feel like I have a big responsibility to ensure my kids can connect to culture and can continue to share their history and be the storytellers for the next generation."

BATTLING THE (MENTAL) DEMONS

One year into a multi-million dollar contract to play AFL football, a fiancée who graced the catwalks of the fashion world ... Buddy Franklin seemed to have the world at his feet at the beginning of 2015.

But his demons were bubbling away beneath the surface. By the end of the football season, he had called "time out" as his team, the Sydney Swans, entered the 2015 finals series. He would not be in their line-up.

Franklin undoubtedly was Sydney's most valuable player and the Swans would need him up front to be a serious finals contender in their sixth straight appearance in the September "big dance."

But Buddy Franklin didn't feel quite right.

His particular demon was mental illness, something that has become better known and more widely recognised as having a real impact on many more people than would have been thought possible just a decade or two previously.

If someone back in the 1980s mentioned mental illness, the first thought was of a brain injury from accident or violence. Possibly birth defects.

But we now know, thanks to high-profile people such as Buddy Franklin and many others, that it runs much deeper than that. Franklin's issue was said to be depression, now recognised as one of the key factors in mental health.

Experts say there are five major categories of mental illnesses:

- Anxiety disorders.
- Mood disorders.
- Schizophrenia and psychotic disorders.
- Dementia.
- Eating disorders.

One aspect of mental health that has alarmed the sport industry and focussed its attention is brain damage through head knocks. From American football, where players wear helmets, to all four football codes that are played widely throughout Australia and many other countries, knocks to the head are now a major concern.

The Harvard Medical School (United States) reported in 2017 there was growing evidence linking football and brain disease.

In Australia, concussion became a major discussion point for all football codes. Such was the concern that rules were introduced to try to limit risks to players who suffered concussion, given that head knocks were part and parcel of every code.

The Australian Football League's concussion guidelines say the minimum timeframe in which a player can return to play in community football is on the 12th day after the day on which the concussion was suffered, based on successfully completing the phases to return to play and receiving a medical clearance.

AFL Chief Medical Officer, Peter Harcourt, said: "The focus must be on ensuring that players pass through each of the steps safely (i.e. rest, recovery and a graded return), without a recurrence of symptoms, rather than simply progressing through a schedule."

But mental illness doesn't always begin with physical injury or trauma.

Back to Buddy Franklin.

Franklin's mental illness wasn't pinned down to concussion. He suffered depression but was brave enough to put his hand up near the end of the 2015 season and seek help.

"It was a tough time for myself leading into the finals. I was really struggling," Franklin said.

"I put my hand up and said I needed help and I'm so glad I did it. I did that, I took some time away and it was the best decision I've made.

"The best thing that I've done is put my hand up to get the help that I needed. And that's the biggest thing for anyone to do, to put your hand up and go, 'yeah I need the help'."

He spoke to *Sydney Swans TV* about his experience. He attributed much of his recovery to his support network, particularly then fiancée Jesinta Campbell (now his wife).

"I've got such a great support network around me in my partner and family and friends, the football club have been terrific in this tough time and I couldn't be more thankful." Franklin said.

With prominent people such as Buddy Franklin talking about mental health, the world has come to recognise just what impact those issues can have.

Many elite sportspeople have spoken about mental health and their experiences: AFL players Nat Fyfe, Tom Boyd, Majak Daw, Wayne Schwass, and Danny Frawley are among those who have shed light on what the affects of mental health can be, So, too, have other prominent Australian sportspeople; swimmer Ian Thorpe, tennis star Nick Kyrgios. netballer Sharni Norder, NRL player Joel Thompson, athlete Morgan Mitchell and swimmer Libby Trickett among them.

On the world sporting stage those who have "put their hand up" include swimmer Michael Phelps, tennis players Naomi Osaka and Serna Williams, gymnast Aly Raisman, skier Lindsey Vonn, wrestler and actor Dwayne "The Rock" Johnson and boxer Frank Bruno. They all have also helped break down the stigma of a condition that for many years wasn't even properly recognised let alone spoken about.

Of course, many outside playing fields have also been affected, and their plight often goes unnoticed. It is the prominence of sportspeople that helps bring such issues to public attention and raises awareness. Prominent sports people have the added stresses of social media coverage.

Athletes often are subjected to offensive, threatening and derogatory remarks by social media users.

The Mental Health Foundation noted: "As much as social media can help with athletes' career and image, it can destroy it just as quickly – and that's tragic. Social media induced stress is dangerous. Not only does it create needless tension, anxiety and sometimes fear triggered by trolling, intimidation, attacks, and threats, but it can affect the athlete's loved ones."

Three times Melbourne Cup winning jockey Glen Boss was one star to speak about mental issues.

Boss told the Asian Racing Conference in Melbourne in February 2023: "I never showed any sign of weakness, or put my hand up looking for help. I was crumbling, I was falling part. I would keep putting up more walls to make myself look stronger... I was so scared, I was in such a dark place."

Fremantle's Nat Fyfe has spoken at some length about the effect of mental demons, anxiety and depression.

Fyfe, twice a Brownlow Medal winner and captain of the Fremantle Dockers for six seasons, revealed how he hit "rock bottom" and battled mental health issues through 2022 after his body broke down and he struggled to get on the field. He played just seven games for the season. He suffered shoulder, back and hamstring injuries.

In an interview after he handed over the captaincy at the

start of 2023, the 32-year-old Fyfe said he had now "come out the other side."

"I had to really go to hell and back with my mental game on my goalkicking because it became quite a burden to step out there in front of goals," he said.

The run of injuries was a reflection of his mental health.

"It was probably the most profound experience of my adult life, to be honest," he said.

"What was happening on the outside, which was injuries, was just a small reflection of what was going on inside.

"I had a fair bit to deal with. I had a good hard look at some of the ailments that we all face as humans in life, in terms of anxiety, depression and a bunch of those internal emotional things, which then came out as injuries.

"I had the shoulder that failed, then I got an infection, then I did my back, then I did multiple hamstrings.

"Internally I was cooked and I was just fighting my way through it, and I just kept breaking down."

The 209-game veteran described his experiences throughout 2022 as a "profound teaching environment" that made him more resilient as he prepared for his 14th season at elite level.

"If you can go through that, find resilience out of it, come out the other side, I feel like that's the juice I now need for the backend of my career," Fyfe said.

"The past accolades were getting stale. There's only so long that you can parrot that you're a two-time Brownlow medallist from years ago.

"They were starting to get stale and I had no juice and motivation out of them, so a good hard look at rock bottom has fired me back up again."

One aspect of his game that suffered noticeably was his

goalkicking. He said he was testing new training techniques to improve his accuracy.

"It's my ultimate strength when I get it all lined up but it can tear me apart when it doesn't quite work," Fyfe said.

"I'm working with a couple of different people more around connecting with that sort of inner voice and that fear, the stress, and getting a good handle on how you can put yourself in the optimal mindset and position to take the shot."

Fyfe said he developed a more positive outlook and hoped some of the worst experiences of his career would help motivate him moving forward.

Most likely Buddy Franklin could identify with Fyfe's experience, he, too, having found a new lease on football life after battling the demons.

Depression is a complex disease. No one has pinned its cause down precisely, although a variety of reasons have been cited. It may affect people in different ways. Some people have depression during a serious medical illness. Others may have depression with life changes such as a move or the death of a loved one. Still others have a family history of depression.

Those who suffer from depression may feel overwhelmed with sadness and loneliness for no known reason.

Buddy Franklin concedes he is not a great communicator but sharing his mental health struggle was the turning point in moving into the next stage of his life; marriage, children, and of course his record-breaking efforts on football fields.

Before taking leave from the game just before the 2015 AFL finals series Franklin said he had felt inhibited and embarrassed to open up about it.

Franklin, who has mild epilepsy, suffered a seizure in public that required urgent medical attention. Epilepsy wasn't directly linked to his mental health issue, but it helped draw attention to the health problems that can afflict people, even those prominent in sport.

Some of Australia's greatest sportspeople have suffered epilepsy throughout their playing careers.

Rugby league player, one of the greatest of all time, Wally Lewis was among them. "Epilepsy affected the last third of my career," Lewis has said.

"I used to have this fear of having a seizure in front of the media, or the players, or the public. I knew it was going to happen, and it did."

Former Socceroos captain Paul Wade also kept his condition secret as a player. Cricket legend and long-time Channel 9 commentator Tony Greig is another who suffered from seizures. So, too was South African cricketer Jonty Rhodes.

Buddy Franklin's condition has been described as a mild form and like other prominent sportspeople it has had a minimal effect on his career.

It is a different story for mental health problems.

Franklin said after revealing he had problems: "It had been an issue for a little while with me, but... I wasn't able to talk about it and I was a little bit embarrassed about it. But for me, being able to speak to the football club, my partner and my family was the best decision I ever made," Franklin told Channel Seven as he prepared to return for the 2016 season.

"At that stage not playing finals football was disappointing, but I'm so glad I did it. I feel much better about myself now and things are looking up," he said.

Although Franklin hasn't pin-pointed his specific triggers, the pressure of playing sport at an elite level for more than 12 years was bound to have had an effect.

"I don't want to go into the details of what went on; that is private. Yes I've come out and said I had mental health issues ... [but] I don't want to go into the details about it [his treatment], I just want to play football, he said after a year off," he said in an interview in 2016.

"In 12 years of football, this is my 12th season, I'd never actually had a proper break. So for me the last two months before getting back to training, I actually needed that break to mentally and physically get myself right... I've never actually had that break and really used it."

Franklin said he couldn't estimate how prevalent mental health issues were among AFL players. "But in the general public, I think one in five people get touched at some stage," he said.

The Australian Bureau of Statistics report on a national study of health and wellbeing 2020-21 highlighted these numbers:

- Over two in five Australians aged 16-85 years (43.7% or 8.6 million people) had experienced a mental disorder at some time in their life
- One in five (21.4% or 4.2 million people) had a 12-month mental disorder
- Anxiety was the most common group of 12-month mental disorders (16.8% or 3.3 million people)
- Almost two in five people (39.6%) aged 16-24 years had a 12-month mental disorder

Franklin said: "The biggest thing for me has been being able to talk about it. And being open and honest with my loved ones and people around me, my family and the football club through this tough period."

With a run of football injuries over his career, his mental health battle gave rise to speculation his career might be over prematurely.

Retirement was "never a factor," he said going into 2016. He had to deal with his issues.

"It was completely switching off and it was all about me. It wasn't about anyone else, just about what I needed to work on," he said. He was aware of the speculation and rumours that swirled around.

"But at the end of the day, for me it was just about getting myself right, getting on the front foot and getting the help I needed, and I was able to do that," he said.

Then-partner Jesinta Campbell said: "There have been some people in the media that have just said some really incredibly nasty and hurtful things that are just so left of field and so wrong in this day and age."

In the 2016 season, Franklin copped sledging from a GWS opponent about his break from the game. He was able to cope, but it was unpleasant.

Beyond Blue founder and former Hawthorn club president Jeff Kennett, said Franklin's announcement that he was dealing with mental health issues "moved the goalposts" in Australia accepting mental illness as a legitimate ailment.

Franklin being comfortable missing a final due to poor mental health was "sad", yet "wonderful".

"This just shows you how tremendously we have moved the goalposts after the last 10 years," Mr Kennett told *New Daily* back in 2015.

"Ten years ago... many would have admitted to their illness after they'd stopped playing, many would have continued playing while ill, which only made the condition worse.

"It is a sad day, for Buddy and the Sydney Swans.

"But it is a wonderful day in clearly illustrating how much we've changed the goalposts in terms of mental illness in Australia."

The Australian Football League Players association also has moved to support players with mental health issues.

The AFLPA developed wellbeing programs including workshops, campaigns and projects, with the focus on collectively building player wellbeing, resilience, and performance as people.

The program includes: mental health education; wellbeing workshops; MindMax resilience; player resilience profiling; social media; gambling harm prevention and practical mindfulness.

The AFLPA's "Brain-based Mental Health" initiative in 2017 is delivered to AFL club staff, players and media. The eight-hour certificate program aims to build mental health awareness and literacy by introducing participants to three core themes; understanding, recognising and managing mental health issues.

The 2015 season saw Hawthorn win their 13th premiership. Sydney after finishing fourth in the home-and-away season bowed out of the finals, losing first to minor premiers Fremantle, then to North Melbourne. Fremantle didn't progress much further either, eliminated in their next game by Hawthorn which went on to defeat West Coast in the Grand final.

Buddy hadn't had a good season from the outset. he had crashed Jesinta's car in April while driving down New South Head Road in Rose Bay, Sydney. No one was injured.

On the field, it became the first time he hadn't kicked 50 goals. He was hit by injury as well as his mental health issues.

An epileptic seizure in a Bondi (Sydney) café saw him taken to hospital. It was a mild episode but nevertheless he was in no fit state to take the field for finals on top of everything else he was going through.

A Swans statement said: "After careful consideration, the club can confirm that Lance Franklin suffers mild epilepsy – unrelated to the current mental health issues he is dealing with."

His coach John Longmire said: "The best place for him now is where he is at the moment and we're right behind him, we support him fully and footy is the last thing on his mind.

"It has been an ongoing issue for a while with Lance but these things are very private.

"It is a condition that is very treatable, but he needs time to be able to treat it and that is what we are giving him.

"He wants people to know about it and understand what he is going through."

Franklin took the last few months of the year away from football to recharge. It was his first real break in more than a decade.

He returned for the start of the 2016 season in good shape.

Some false information doing the rounds in the coverage of his situation was secondary, Franklin said, but still unpleasant.

"For me, I've been used to it for a number of years. There are a lot of rumours that go around about me, a lot of things I can't control. But I did feel sorry for my loved ones, my partner, my parents and the football club at that stage with the stuff that was getting thrown around.

"But at the end of the day, for me it was just about getting myself right, getting on the front foot and getting the help I needed, and I was able to do that."

He said going public about his condition was the best decision he ever made.

His message: "If you are struggling, I definitely recommend that you ask for that help, because it will change your life, definitely."

FIRST NATIONS AT THE FOREFRONT

BOLAND, BARTY... AND OF COURSE, BUDDY

Australia warmly celebrates its First Nations sport stars; rightly so. There have been First Nations and Torres Strait Islander champions in a wide range of sports; athletics, all football codes, boxing, basketball, netball, hockey, horse racing and many others.

The 3-Bs hailed for their efforts in 2022 are A-grade performers no matter how you look at their record-breaking careers.

Ash Barty bowed out of tennis as world No.1 and a twice Grand Slam winner. Scott Boland burst on to the Test Cricket scene with an 18-wicket haul against the "old enemy" England in the 2021-22 series. Buddy Franklin became just the sixth player – and first First Nations player – in 100 years of the game to kick 1,000 career goals.

Just as Australians are proud of them and their achievements, they are equally as proud of their heritage.

Scott Boland and Ash Barty didn't know about their First Nations heritage immediately but embraced it enthusiastically when they traced it back a couple of generations.

Buddy Franklin's indigenous history has been more familiar to him; his mother is a First Nations woman. He, too, has embraced his heritage enthusiastically.

SCOTT BOLAND got the ball rolling, pretty much literally, in his debut in the Australian cricket team in the last week of 2021 and into 2022. He made a record-breaking start to his Test career in the Third Test against England at the MCG.

In 2017, Scott Boland's family discovered that his grandfather, John Edward, was a First Nations man, from the Gulidjan tribe in the Colac area of Victoria. Boland, then in his mid-20s, sought to embrace his heritage, playing in First Nations representative teams, and seeking to further educate himself on traditions.

In 2018, Boland was selected in the Aboriginal XI that toured England to celebrate the 150th anniversary of the 1868 Aboriginal team that travelled to England. His brother Nick was also in the squad of 13.

In 2021 he went into the Australian Test team to replace injured captain Pat Cummins.

Technically, he became the best bowler in Test history – sort of – among cricketers who had taken more than 10 Test wickets. The Victorian seamer cemented his place in Ashes folklore by claiming 6 for 7 on Test debut at the MCG in December 2021.

He played in the three final Tests of the Ashes series, taking 18 wickets at an average of 9.55, as Australia won the five-Test series 4-0, with one Test drawn.

Sports journalist Ron Reed wrote in *Captain Pat – Cometh the hours Cummins the Man* (Wilkinson publishing): "Selected out of the blue for the iconic Boxing Day Test at the MCG, Boland immediately became a matchwinner, taking seven wickets for the match, including six for seven in the second innings – the sort of figures you might only ever see in scorebooks devoted to young kids in the park –and was instantly hailed as the newest hero of Australian sport.

"It wasn't just because of his performance – as monumental as that was – but every bit as importantly, he had just become only the second Indigenous male, and the fourth of either gender, to play Test cricket for Australia."

Boland didn't play another Test until late in 2022 when he was called up to the Australian team for the second Test against the West Indies in Adelaide in December, again replacing the injured skipper. That gave him the chance to add to the 18 wickets he took during the Ashes series against England the previous Australian summer.

He did just that, spectacularly, taking 3-16 from 10 overs in the West Indies second innings as Australia won the Test by 419 runs and claim the series 2-0. Boland followed Jason Gillespie to become the second First Nations Australian to play Test cricket.

He retained his place at the start of the next series on home turf, against South Africa and after two Tests boasted a record of 48 overs, 7 for 125 as Australia took an unassailable 2-0 lead in the series heading into 2023.

ASH BARTY found out about her First Nations heritage when she was seven years old. It came from her father Robert's side of the family. Her paternal great-grandmother was of the Ngaragu people.

Barty rose to World No.1 in women's tennis in 2021, winning Wimbledon and backing up with another Grand Slam title, the Australian Open, early in 2022, before retiring on top of the world in March, aged just 26. Then came new ventures, marriage and the announcement in January 2023 that she was expecting a baby, news warmly welcomed by her fans.

She had talked about her heritage while on the world circuit: "My heritage is really important to me," she said. "I've always had that olive complexion and the squished nose, and I just think its important to do the best I can to be a good role model."

As she bowed out, her Women's Tennis Association record was: Highest ranking, No.1; $US 23,879,070 prizemoney; 15

singles titles; win/loss record of 305/102. Though retired since early in 2022, she was still collecting accolades at the end of the year, awarded her fifth consecutive John Newcombe Medal at the Australian Tennis Awards.

Her father Rob was 13 years old when he was told by a cousin he had First Nations heritage, something his parents denied, insisting the family had links to Maoris in New Zealand.

"To his parents, Aboriginal ancestry was something to be ashamed of and not something to be curious about," Ash wrote in her book, *My Dream Time*.

At 17, Rob had pieced together his family tree, confirming that he was a Ngarigo man. He found out his great-grandmother Nancy was a First Nations Australian. The Ngaragu people were from southern New South Wales and north-eastern Victoria.

Ash Barty followed in the footsteps of another First Nations Australian, Evonne Cawley (Gooloogong) to star in world tennis.

Ash revealed that racism had raised its head during her career.

"I've seen glimpses and tasted the faintest bitter edge of racism. I'd win a Deadly Award (national Aboriginal and Torres Strait Islander acievement awards) but get vilified online. I'd become a Tennis Australia First Nations Ambassador and then find some muppet calling my heritage into question," she wrote in her book.

"I've been lucky to have so many incredible role models who have paved a path for me to believe, as a First Nations woman, that I am capable of anything."

BUDDY FRANKLIN's heritage through his mother is via the Noongar-Whadjuk people.

The Noongar people have lived in the south-west corner of Western Australia for at least 45,000 years. There are several language groups that make up the Noongar, including the Whadjuk, who are the traditional owners of the land around Perth.

Before the arrival of Europeans, the Noongar population was estimated at between 6,000 and some tens of thousands.

Buddy honours his heritage with frequent visits to First Nations communities. He and four other Swans players – Braeden Campbell, Will Gould, Hayden McLean and Sam Wicks – visited Darwin and the Maningrida community in November 2022 to raise awareness for rheumatic heart disease and scabies and meet children at a local school.

"It's always good to get back to Alice Springs, Darwin, there's so many Aboriginals up here, I give back to the kids because I remember being their age and seeing West Coast Eagles players coming to the communities I was at, it's something that you never forget, it's always good giving back to the community," Buddy said.

"AFL is one of the best jobs you can have, I remember the boys saying don't worry it will go quickly, which it surely has but I've enjoyed every minute of it."

He celebrated his 1,000th goal in March 2022 by draping the First Nations flag over himself.

Buddy's wife Jesinta, shares his passion for First Nations issues, and has spoken out against Australia Day celebrations and the mistreatment of people in custody.

She wrote an article for *Stellar* magazine in 2020 explaining why she refused to celebrate Australia Day on 26 January.

"I have seen my husband well-up when talking about his mum (Ursula) and how she used to have to run away with her siblings when they knew the government trucks were coming to take them away from their parents," she wrote in reference to the Stolen Generations.

Franklin moved with his parents and three older sisters to the small town of Dowerin, north-east of Perth, when he was young and for a time lost touch with his mother's family.

"As I've matured I've got to know a lot more about that side of the family," he said in an interview with the *Daily Telegraph*.

"But going to the bush like we did, I didn't get to see them that much."

"There were difficult times at school being the only Indigenous kid there," he said. "But I had my family for support and I had my four sisters, I was the baby boy. But I think there are a lot of challenges growing up.

"I was fortunate to have great support from my mum and dad. Without them there is no way I would have gotten there."

Franklin joined a long list of First Nations Australians to make their mark in Australian Rules football. Team lists from 2007 to 2022 contained 72 players of First Nations heritage, 10% of all players.

So who is the greatest of all time?

An impressive list of candidates have graced the fields of VFL/AFL competitions since Doug Nicholls (later Sir Douglas) became the first First Nations man to try out for the top level of what was then the VFL.

Sir Douglas made a huge impact on the VFL. playing for North Melbourne and then Carlton. In 1932 he played for Fitzroy and in 1934 came third in the Brownlow Medal count. In 1935, he was the first Aboriginal man to be selected for a Victorian Interstate Team. In 1972, he was knighted for work as a player, Christian Worker (he was Pastor Doug Nicholls at that time) and South Australian Governor. He was the first First Nations man to be knighted.

It is worth looking at the career of Doug Nicholls in a little more depth, as he paved the way for some many others, from football to First Nations advancement (Aboriginal Advancement as it then was). Nicholls , from the Yorta Yorta people, was born on 9 December 1906 on the Cummeragunja Reserve in NSW, the youngest of five children. After playing in the Goulburn Valley for Tongala, Nicholls tried out for VFL clubs North Melbourne and Carlton before the 1927 season.

He played some seconds matches for Carlton but did not play a senior game, leaving after being ostracised (for his colour). He then joined the Northcote Football Club in the VFA where he made his name as a speedy wingman.

He was one of the shortest players in the game at the time, but his speed was unmatched. He was a member of Northcote's 1929 premiership team, and finished third in the Recorder Cup voting in 1931, his final season with Northcote.

In 1932, Nicholls joined Fitzroy Football Club in the VFL. He was chosen for Victoria four times. He played six seasons for Fitzroy, before returning to Northcote in 1938 until knee injuries forced him to retire in 1939. He returned to Northcote as non-playing coach in 1947.

Nicholls also was capable sprinter. He competed in Gift races around Victoria and in 1928 he won the Nyah and Warracknabeal Gifts. Race organisers then paid him an appearance fee, board and expenses to enter races.

He was the inaugural chairman of the National Aboriginal Sports Foundation.

To earn a living during the football off-season, Nicholls boxed with Jimmy Sharman's Boxing Troupe, a travelling sideshow in which Sharman's fighters took on challenges from all-comers.

He enlisted in the CMF during World WarII and organised and captained First Nations teams in football matches in patriotic fundraisers.

He was a founding member of the Aborigines Advancement League in Victoria and became Governor of South Australia in December 1976 until a stroke forced him to step down. He was awarded the OBE and MBE in Australian honours.

A federal elctorate is named Nicholls in his honour. He died in 1988 at Mooroopna, Victoria.

In 2016, the AFL began honouring Nicholls by naming the annual Indigenous Round after him.

Many First Nations players followed him into the VFL, and more recently, the AFL.

It is an impressive list. These are just some from the last few decades; Graeme "Polly" Farmer, Barry Cable, Adam Goodes, Andrew Mcleod, Peter Matera, Stephen Michael, Cyril and Maurice Rioli, Gavin Wanganeen, Nicky Winmar, Eddie Betts, Michael O'Loughlin, Michael Long, Syd Jackson, Jeff Farmer, Byron Pickett, Jim Krakouer, Peter Burgoyne, David Wirrpanda, Chris Lewis.

So where would Buddy Franklin rate among that list of stars?

AFL legend and commentator Kevin Bartlett says it's hard to look past Lance Franklin as the greatest First Nations AFL player of all time. That's probably a discussion that's been had and will be had again.

THE ELEPHANT IN THE ROOM

Racism issues have always been bubbling just below the surface of the AFL competition for decades.

That's not to say racism in sport is exclusive to football. There have been many incidents in all codes of football; even golf and tennis have seen it.

The AFL has tried to get on the front foot by developing a comprehensive policy aimed at stamping out racism: "The AFL strongly condemns racial vilification in the football community including our players, staff, and their families, across all levels of our game," CEO Gillon McLachlan said in 2021 when re-stating the policy designed to protect "Aboriginal and Islander" players.

The AFL's original Racial and Religious Vilification Policy introduced in the mid-2000s was an Australian first, and sent a strong message that the game was taking a stand against racism.

One round of the competition each year is named after former players and leading advocate for First Nations interest, Sir Douglas Nicholls, to promote the game's inclusiveness.

Racism incidents, however, continued, with a number of players subjected to abuse, mostly from spectators.

In 1993 at Victoria Park St Kilda star Neil "Nicky" Winmar famously responded to racist abuse from the Collingwood crowd by lifting his shirt after the game and pointing with pride to his dark skin.

Sydney Swans' Adam Goodes took a strong stand against racism, which led to him regularly being racially abused and booed at matches.

In May 2013, Goodes spoke about the racial taunts he experienced, particularly in his years as a Swan: "I felt like I was in high school again, being bullied, being called all these names because of my appearance. I didn't stand up for myself in high school – I'm a lot more confident, I'm a lot more proud about who I am, and my culture, and I decided to stand up last night, and I'll continue to stand up."

The 2013 incident he referred to involved a 13-year-old girl in the crowd calling the Swans forward an "ape". Goodes had had enough – he stood in front of the girl, pointed her out to security and she was escorted from the ground. Goodes said he was not blaming the girl, saying after she later phoned him to apologise that she deserved to be supported and educated about why the racist comment was unacceptable.

Goodes' worst experiences of racism were between 2013 and 2015.

He said, "As a kid we moved around a fair bit as a family. It was difficult to make friends but sport helped. Once people saw you kick a football it broke down barriers. Instead of being the new skinny black kid you were the kid everyone wanted on their team. That really helped break those barriers as we moved from one small country town to another. The football field was a place where I could express myself and just be me. Play the game as well as you can and that's what you're judged on. Not the colour of your skin, or your beliefs, or the conversation you have around racism."

Throughout his last season, Goodes was constantly booed, sort of herd mentality. In 2014, Goodes and new teammate Lance Franklin both were subjected to racist comments by a member of the crowd when the Swans played the Bulldogs in Melbourne.

Neither player heard the comments during the game at Etihad Stadium, but police confirmed a Bulldogs supporter was removed from the ground for racially vilifying the two. Other spectators pointed out the person who had made the remarks.

"It's disappointing that it's still happening in the community and especially at football games," Franklin said. "It's obviously very good that the crowd has come forward and spoken up.

"I think it's just something that needs to be cut out of the game and the more we can teach people not to be racist, the better for the game."

In June 2019 the Australian Football League (AFL) and its 18 clubs apologised unreservedly to Goodes for failing to support him adequately in the face of abuse.

It was widely reported that the decision by Goodes to retire in 2015 was mostly because of the racism to which he had been subjected over his 17 seasons as a player.

Go to 2022, and the AFL was rocked by serious – shocking might be a better word – allegations involving coaching staff at Hawthorn Football Club. Two coaches at the time who were named in the allegations denied any wrong-doing. The AFL set up an independent inquiry.

The Hawthorn club launched an internal review. The club also was embroiled in a muddy board election that saw former premiership player Andy Gowers (endorsed by the "Hawks for Change") group elected president on a mandate for change at the club.

Gowers did not want to immediately comment on the racism allegations: "I'm not going to say or do anything that's going to jeopardise the process that's underway now by the AFL independent panel," he said. "It's just not appropriate."

The allegations of mistreatment of First Nations players and their families involved incidents between 2008 and 2016.

A group of First Nations families agreed to take part in the independent investigation into allegations on the basis the AFL commissioned a separate independent review of the league's "own failings." Hawthorn's own inquiry made no adverse findings, prompting the AFL to launch a new inquiry in June 2023.

The allegations grabbed the headlines in the lead-up to the 2022 AFL grand final between the Sydney Swans and Geelong.

Swans star Franklin was at Hawthorn at the time of the alleged incidents, in which unidentified First Nations players claimed the AFL club demanded they separate from their partners, and pressured one couple to terminate a pregnancy for the sake of the player's career.

Franklin had just signed a one-year extension with the Swans to extend his playing career and preferred to focus on the upcoming decider. While he did not get involved in the 2022 controversy he had previously been vocal about racism.

In 2020, he joined other thousands of sportspeople in protesting against racism across the world after the killing of George Floyd, an African-American man who died when a white police officer knelt down on his neck for almost nine minutes.

Floyd's cries of "I can't breathe" was adopted as a symbol for anti-racism protests around the world. Participants in a wide variety of sports adopted "taking a knee" (kneeling down) at the start of games as support for anti-racism action.

Franklin was asked what it was like to be on the field with Goodes during the booing he was subjected to in 2015.

"For me personally when I heard the booing it was pretty sad really," he said. "To see Goodesy that upset, it was hard. It was hard for all the boys and we just had to be there to support him through it."

He was asked if the racist overtones of the booing had a personal impact? "It was affecting Adam, so I stand by Goodesy," he said.

"He was upset he was getting booed. I was upset by it and the football club was there to support him."

Franklin also has been the subject of vilification from football crowds, at an AFL match in Launceston in 2011, in particular.

Playing for Hawthorn against the West Coast, a male fan called Franklin a "black ****" several times, among other derogatory comments.

It's understood the abuse began early in the game and continued throughout the match. Franklin expressed disbelief at the comments directed at him.

Franklin, reluctant to speak publicly about such incidents, told close friends he preferred not to be central to racism issues, but said he shouldn't be subjected to racial abuse from spectators.

The Hawks were told of the incident after the game – by a teammate of Franklin. Officials spoke to Franklin.

"It's disappointing that after much positive work has been done to stamp out this kind of behaviour that we still have to deal with the issue of racism in sport," a Hawks spokesman said.

"We don't condone this kind of behaviour at any level of the game."

The media is not free from blame in dealing adversely with First Nations issues. Jesinta Franklin was asked by an interviewer on Sydney radio if Franklin was "half or is he full Aboriginal".

While at Hawthorn, Franklin travelled to Darwin and Alice Springs visiting First Nations communities.

He spoke in a media interview about how First Nations players inspired youngsters: "When you see Aboriginal and Torres Strait Islanders play well, being a kid from the bush it gives you something to strive for," he said.

"For me, it made me want to work harder to achieve my goals. Football is what I always wanted to do and every training session I train my heart out and I try my hardest every weekend."

Those who inspired him? He named Goodes and Adelaide champion Andrew McLeod. "To see those guys be successful was really good," he said.

COME IN NO. 23

If you play sport and wear the No. 23 you are in the company of some of the world's elite athletes. Think of basketballer Michael Jordan, Australian Test cricket hero Shane Warne, British soccer player David Beckham.

Such is the fame of some of the world's No. 23s that the number often was retired after the player had retired.

Buddy Franklin wore No. 23 at Hawthorn and retained it when he joined Sydney.

Hawthorn placed much significance in its No. 23 jumper. It was never awarded lightly.

Ashley Browne writing for *hawthornfc.com.au* in 2011, "You have to be tough. You have to be brave. You have to inspire. You have to be capable of the freakish and be able to win game, sometimes off your own booth if that is what I takes."

More than 20 Hawthorn players have worn No, 23 over the years but Browne's description seems to fit none better than Buddy Franklin.

Of course mention should be made of some other great No. 23s with the Hawks: John Peck, Don Scott and Dermott Brereton.

The number has been significant in several AFL clubs: Andrew McLeod at Adelaide, Justin Leppitsch at Brisbane, Stewart Loewe at St Kilda, David Dench at North Melbourne are just a few. It would be a fair team of No. 23s. No. 23 has been worn in the AFL by two Brownlow Medallists, two Norm Smith Medallists and nine Coleman Medallists

The first notable No. 23 at Hawthorn was ruckman/defender Ted Fletcher, who played 129 games from 1948-54.

After Dermot Brereton left the Hawks in 1993, the jumper was given to Michael Collica and Nathan Thompson, among others.

The Hawks switched Franklin from No. 38 to No. 23 in his second season (2006).

When Buddy left for Sydney at the end of 2012, the Hawks gave the number to key-position player Tim O'Brien.

At the Swans, Buddy took over the No. 23 jumper from Jordan Lockyer.

"I'm super excited to wear the number 23," Franklin told the club's website. "I wore it for a number of years at Hawthorn, so to get the number here at Sydney is something that I'm looking forward to wearing."

Lockyer conceded he'd become attached to the No. 23 which he had chosen when he joined the Swans

"I was a bit hesitant to give up the number, but after speaking to Lance and speaking to others at the footy club, I'm now really excited about wearing the number 18," he said – a number he wore as a junior player.

The most famous player in world sport to wear it was superstar Chicago Bulls bastketballer Michael Jordan, recognised widely as the greatest of all time.

Jordan wore No. 23 because of his brother, not some superstition, significant event or even Chinese mythology.

Larry Jordan was said to be the better basketballer when the two were young. Michael's first preference was baseball.

When they were on the same team in high school, elder

brother Larry wore number 45. Michael chose half of 45, 22.5 and rounded it up to 23, so the legend goes.

Other basketball greats who attained fame in the No 23 include LeBron James and Anthony Davis, all Hall of Fame-level players.

It has been a famous number in other sports in the US.

Major League Baseball: Don Mattingly, Ryne Sandberg, and Zach Greinke.

NFL Football: Troy Vincent, Patrick Surtain, Mike Wagner, Devin Hester. Dave Whitsell, Brig Owens.

NHL Hockey: Bob Gainey, Brian Bellows, Milan Hejduk, Bob Nystrom, Eddie Shack

Outside the US, many famous sportspeople have worn No. 23.

Soccer: David Beckham (Real Madrid), Sol Campbell, Jamie Carragher.

Cricket: Shane Warne, Michael Clarke, Kuldeep Yadhav.

FOOTNOTE:

Mathematicians and data scientists have been investigating the number 23 for many years.

Number 23 was important to numerous religions including Christianity and Islam.

In Christianity, Psalm 23, also known as the Shepherd's Psalm, is possibly the best-known psalm.

The Qur'an was revealed over 23 years to the prophet Muhammed. Muslims believe that the first verses of the Qur'an were revealed to Muhammad on the 23rd night of the 9th Islamic month.

According to the birthday paradox, in a group of 23 (or more) randomly chosen people, the probability is more than 50% that some pair of them will have the same birthday. A related coincidence is that 365 times the natural logarithm of 2, which is approximately 252.999, is very close to the number of pairs of 23 items, 253.

Number twenty-three is also in the human body and genes. Normal human sex cells have 23 chromosomes. Other human cells have 46 chromosomes, arranged in 23 pairs. The average human physical biorhythm is 23 days and the blood circulates the body on average every 23 seconds.

There are two movies about number 23 called *The Number 23.* In 2007, Jim Carrey played a man obsessed with the 23 enigma in the movie. And the German production movie called *23* was also about a man obsessed with the number.

According to interetsingengineering.com, John Forbes Nash, American Nobel Prize-winning mathematician and the subject of the movie *A Beautiful Mind,* was obsessed with 23. He believed that the number 23 has a unique role in human relationships, for personal health and the life order; it had a special significance for his work. Interestingly, Nash has published 23 scientific articles during his life. He died on 23 May, 2015.

Trivia

Nissan typically uses No. 23 for their Motorsport manufacturer teams, as the numbers 2 and 3 are pronounced "ni" and "san" in Japanese.

BEHIND THE HEADLINES

Maybe it is tall poppy syndrome. Maybe it is just that some people like to find fault in people at the expense of seeing the good things.

Sunday Herald Sun columnist David Penberthy summed it up well: "When it comes to those in the public eye, especially those as comparatively affluent as Franklin, there is an added and perverse 'let it rip' quality which informs the debate around well-known figures."

As if signing a $10 million 9-year deal with the Sydney Swans in 2013 wasn't big enough news, the gossips and media went into overdrive in April 2014 when Franklin crashed then-girlfriend Jesinta's car in swanky Rose Bay on 23 April.

Buddy, who was just setting out on his lucrative deal with the Swans, fronted the media the next morning and apologised for the crash in which five cars were badly damaged, including the one he was driving.

As is practice he was breath-tested, NSW police confirming a negative result. Buddy was not required to attend court over the infringement notice.

Yet all sorts of speculation emerged, just as they had when paramedics were called to his unit only weeks earlier. That incident turned out to be epilepsy-related (as was his collapse at a Bondi café a year later.)

Buddy and the Swans quickly laid to rest questions about the Rose Bay accident.

"I'm truly sorry for the inconvenience cause to other people's cars," Franklin said.

"This is something that not anyone wants to go through. I don't want to see myself in the spotlight again. The immediate reaction is just shock. I was devastated. I'm just so thankful that no one was in the car with me."

Police confirmed Buddy was the only person involved in the accident, and was unharmed.

A Sydney Swans statement said: "He was not carrying any passengers and there were no passengers in any of the other vehicles involved. No one was injured in the accident."

Franklin said he wasn't on the phone or speeding when he crashed into four parked cars. He was frustrated at being back in the spotlight for another off-field incident.

Speaking before training the next day, Buddy said he didn't see a car parked on the left as he drove through Rose Bay, clipped it and then crashed into the other cars after the airbags went off.

"I wasn't texting at all. I wasn't doing anything. I wasn't speeding. It was just an accident, accidents happen and as I said I'm so grateful that no one was hurt in this case, and for the people's cars that were hit, we can get them fixed up as soon as possible and move on."

Buddy said he was shocked and shaky after the accident, but also annoyed at himself.

"Obviously there's frustration, more for myself than anyone," he said. "I don't want to see myself in the spotlight. Obviously I've found myself in it again but I just want to move forward as quickly as possible and get on to this week's game."

All that came of the incident as far as police were concerned was the issuing of a traffic infringement notice for negligent driving. He was fined $405 and lost three demerit points.

The Jeep he was driving was on loan to Jesinta from Jeep Australia.

Just a month earlier, Buddy was in the news when he lent his Mercedes to teammate Dan Hanneberry who crashed it. Buddy wasn't involved in the accident.

He hadn't much luck on the roads. In 2012, he lost his licence for six months after he was booked for speeding 40km/h over the limit in Melbourne's Brighton East.

Buddy Franklin is one of many of the greats in sport who have found themselves at the centre of controversy.

To be fair, Buddy's outstanding achievements in the AFL have far outshone the shadows some commentary have cast over him during his career. The shadows have been few, but there is no doubt they have hurt.

The most hurtful one probably was to have been labelled a "coward" during an AFL tribunal hearing. Rumours that abounded during his break from football during 2015 probably also cut to the quick, for himself and those close to him.

Media commentators haven't always been in his corner either, not that they have any obligation to be so, but most have been universal in their praise for his achievements. Certainly Buddy's 100 goals haul in a season and 1,000 goals in a career received the accolades they deserved.

But go back to 2015 when Buddy went through a horrible period. He later acknowledged that his mental health was the issue that saw him step away from the game just before the 2015 finals series.

The Sydney Swans club was forced to step in, to put to rest sensational rumours that Franklin had an affair with a teammate's partner. There were also rumours about substances, also without substance of course.

The club revealed Franklin's break from the game was to allow him to deal with mental health issues. He'd also suffered an epileptic seizure in public and had to deal with that.

"There have been some people in the media that have just said some really incredibly nasty and hurtful things that are just so left of field and so wrong in this day and age," future wife Jesinta Campbell said at the time.

Swans general manager of football Tom Harley hit out at the rumours, saying they were completely false.

"We were really transparent... and almost we were compelled to be in regards to the mental health issues that Lance has got and also the epilepsy and there's nothing further to add," Harley said.

"Unfortunately, this time of year being a high-profile player, there is a lot of scuttlebutt and I can pour cold water on all of that. It's absolute rubbish and it's really unsavoury to be honest.

"We really do need to be respectful of the situation at the moment. People need to respect that the club's been really transparent and honest since it came to hand last week. There's nothing further to add."

Collingwood president at the time, Eddie McGuire, said fans need to give Franklin space to deal with his mental health.

"Let's be honest, we've heard them all [the rumours]," McGuire said.

"We've heard the mail on everything that Buddy was doing, all sorts of things. You name anything that could be salacious in regards to this situation and it's been alleged.

"I don't really care if things are happening behind the scenes, the guy is crook at the moment. Let's have some space. We've got plenty of good football to talk about at the moment, so let's park Buddy Franklin for the moment."

Sunday Herald Sun columnist David Penberthy wrote: "He (Franklin) has been the subject of a greater number of rumours about his alleged bad-boy ways. It matters not whether these rumours are true.

"The defining feature of those who spread them is that they almost invariably have no inside knowledge of anything. Yet they are out there in their hundreds and they got another airing this week when the news broke that Buddy would not be playing finals for Sydney this weekend."

Penberthy added: "Franklin is a once-in-a-generation footballer. Both he and the Swans are to be commended for making the decision to go public about his situation. If it means there is one other bloke out there who's battling his own demons, but who through seeing Franklin's admitted vulnerability decides to get help, then that is a terrific thing."

Newspaper columnists seem always to have found Franklin a subject of interest, not always separating the good from the bad,

Peter Fitsimmons (a former rugby union player) writing in the *Sydney Morning Herald* didn't find anything good in the Swans' decision to sign Franklin.

The headline screamed: HAVE THE SWANS GOT FREAKING ROCKS IN THEIR HEAD?

Best to leave it at that.

Then of course there was controversy over a clothing line he put his name to. It wasn't his name that drew the ire of activists, but the use of the First Nations flag.

Australia's first First Nations Olympic gold medallist and former Senator Nova Peris led the charge.

She said Buddy's promotion of the company, which purchased the worldwide licence to use the flag design in 1971, was a "kick in the guts" to the First Nations community.

Buddy was stung by the attack. He promptly announced in a Twitter post that his company would stop ordering or selling the products in question (mostly T-shirts).

"I have been deeply disturbed by comments targeting me about the use of the Aboriginal flag on T-shirts we produced through the only licensed and legal avenue, being through WAM clothing, and in doing so, with full and due respect to the artist, Harold Thomas," his post said.

"Our intention was to produce the T-shirt, as an expression of my cultural pride and to encourage Australians of all backgrounds to wear our flag, that is an official flag of our country, with pride.

"It was never, our intention to disrespect others in Aboriginal communities, and as a result of this issue, we will not be seeking to order or sell any further T-shirts or merchandise until the matter of our flag being made freely available is resolved for the good of our people, and our country."

Perhaps one of the most hurtful episodes for Buddy Franklin came in an appearance before the AFL tribunal in 2022.

He was reported for striking Richmond Captain Trent Cotchin after a clash at the MCG on 28 May.

The report earned a one-match suspension which the Swans appealed on Franklin's behalf. The suspension was upheld but not before some heated exchanges between advocates appearing before the tribunal.

Sydney's counsel Duncan Miller argued Cotchin had "exaggerated" the contact, claiming the Tigers star could earn an invite to the *Logies* rather than the Brownlow Medal. When asked if he meant to strike Cotchin high, Franklin replied: "Absolutely not."

"No way would I ever do that," he said. "It's not in the spirit of the game – I definitely wouldn't have done it."

The AFL' counsel assisting the Tribunal Andrew Woods characterised Franklin's strike on Cotchin as "cowardly."

When details of the comments were revealed, Sydney came out swinging. Swans chairman Andrew Pridham was furious. The club said the AFL had not afforded Franklin the respect he deserved in prosecuting the case, describing Woods' comments as "insulting" and "inappropriate".

Pridham said the AFL had gone over the top in its pursuit of a suspension.

"To question his integrity and to say he's acted in a cowardly way I think is demeaning, inappropriate and inaccurate," he said.

"I think it's extremely disappointing. I think his choice of words were very poor, I think it's inappropriate."

The AFL reacted with a rare public apology for the language used in the Tribunal hearing.

The AFL issued a statement distancing the league from the comments made by Woods, and said "rhetorical flourishes" used by both counsel had no place in tribunal proceedings.

"There are no cowardly players in the AFL, let alone Lance Franklin," the AFL said.

"Lance Franklin is a champion of our game.

"In the making of submissions, legal counsel assisting the tribunal used his own words to describe the circumstances of the strike on Trent Cotchin, namely that Mr Cotchin was reasonably not expecting to be struck by Mr Franklin.

"Trent Cotchin is a premiership captain and one of the most respected leaders in the competition.

"It is the AFL's view that rhetorical flourishes of the nature used by both counsel last night should not be part of the AFL tribunal process and they do not reflect the views of the AFL."

To round off the year, Buddy's "shocker" in the 2022 Grand Final against Geelong thrust him into the unwanted limelight yet again. Social media keyboard warriors fire up with "missing in action" posts prominent.

His sixth Grand Final appearance was one he'd be quick to forget, having just signed for a one-season extension with the Swans,

He was shut out by Geelong defender Jack Henry, managing just one behind from five disposals; his equal-lowest tally since his debut season.

Franklin managed just 2 goals from 23 disposals across three finals matches, with both majors coming in the second quarter of the Swans' preliminary final win over Collingwood.

"Two of his worst games in the whole of his career have come in this finals series," former Port Adelaide player and commentator Kane Corners observed.

His 52 goals from 23 games for the season and becoming just the sixth player in history to reach 1,000 career goals now a distant memory for much of the commentary about his Grand Final performance.

Needless to say, much commentary centred on his just-signed one-year deal with the Swans.

Putting all that behind him and go on to record his 1,000th goal in the AFL took strength of character. As for 2023, coach John Longmire was looking forward to Franklin's contribution, particularly with some up and coming young players around him.

"We were talking to him before Christmas and he's in the best space he's ever been. He loves playing with younger players. He loves seeing young players come through. He smells talent and he identifies it pretty quickly. He knows when kids can and can't play.

"He walks into this building... He just comes up to me with

a smile and says, 'how good is this joint?' For a player that's been around for a long time, I'm pretty sure that Lance won't be out seeking too many headlines this year," Longmire said.

But Longmire said the Swans wouldn't be placing a heavy reliance on Buddy's left boot in 2023. "Lance shouldn't have to be a star performer every year, particularly at 35, 36. I think clearly that's an unrealistic expectation," he said.

"It wouldn't be too much of a surprise to say we don't expect him to play every week, every minute of the game... at 36, it can be a real challenge to do that.

"He hasn't been going at full power through the pre-season, so the plan is to build him up again this week, and it will take a few weeks for him to hit his stride."

Teammate Isaac Heaney was confident buddy could have a big season. "He's obviously had a slow build-up, which he's not necessarily happy about because all he wants to do is get out there and train and play," he said.

"He's looking fit and he's good to go... hopefully he can have that big impact that he's had over the past 18 years.

"I think it's all dependent on his body."

Heeney said he would not be surprised if Franklin continued in 2024.

"But if this is his last season, I'll cherish knowing that I've played with arguably the best player to play the game," he said.

The year ahead was going to be tough for the Swans after the humiliation of the 2022 Grand Final thrashing.

Buddy and his teammates had a point to prove, and a lot could turn on the effectiveness of Buddy's size 13 left boot.

For Buddy there could be more chances for celebration; he started the 2023 season nine short of 350 games, and 33 goals short of becoming the first player to kick 500 goals for two clubs.

Bootnote

Buddy burst out the blocks in his first game of the 2023 season on 18 March, kicking his side's first 2 goals as the Swans dealt with the Gold Coast Suns by 49 points. The Swans became just the second beaten Grand Finalist in seven years to win their opening game of the next season.

The downside was that a clumsy bump late in the match on Sam Collins saw Buddy under scrutiny by the Match Review Officer, resulting in the "offer" of a one-match suspension that cost him an appearance in the Swans' first home game of the year. It also possibly cost Buddy a last hurrah game against his old club, Hawthorn, if 2023 was to be his last season in AFL. He may also have missed out on a bag of goals as the Swans thrashed the hapless Hawks by 81 points and set the early pace on the AFL ladder.

His playing time in the 2023 season would depend on fitness with coach Longmire saying Buddy would be managed carefully, particularly as he suffered an early injury setback.

Buddy put the boots on for his 350th AFL game on Thursday 8 June 2023, against St Kilda at the SCG, after making his debut at that ground on 27 March 2005, playing for Hawthorn against the Swans.

He is the 22nd player to reach 350 games. Coincidentally, he played games 100, 200 and 300 against the Saints.

His word on the milestone: "...when you get to my age, you've got to manage yourself as best as possible and do all the right things to make sure you can get out there."

His 350th game didn't bring joy to Swans fans in terms of a win. But he did mark his likely last career milestone by moving ahead of Doug Wade into fourth on the VFL/AFL all-time goalkickers. His two goals took his career tally to 1,059. Teammates chaired him from the ground to mark his 350th game.

THE VOTES ARE IN

Lance Franklin is a generational footballer, the most dynamic presence on a football field this century. It could safely be argued that he just may be the most dynamic, explosive and effective footballer in living memory.

Some may have been as good, but none have had the longevity. We'll leave the final say on where Franklin stands in the pantheon of goalkicking greats, to those hall-of-fame legends and the goalkicking greats of the game.

Peter McKenna

"I think he's one of the greatest kicks of all time… the distance he can kick is unbelievable… I think he's helped by that arc, that helps him generate power, a little bit like the rugby players when they put the ball down, they come from the angle and swing into the ball."

"He is a sensational kick of the football. One of the best of all time, for sure."

"For a guy of his height, he wasn't a great overhead mark, but his danger has always been on the rebound, when the ball comes loose. Whenever the balls is loose inside 50, he's a danger. His agility for a guy that's 199cm, you have to rate him as one of the greatest forwards ever."

Peter Hudson

"He lights the game up, he's a brilliant player."

"The one thing I find about Buddy that is so unique, is his ability to run, pick up the ball and run around opponents. He'd pick up the ball and he'd have four blokes trying to catch him, the further he went, the further he got away."

Mike Sheahan

(Veteran AFL Journalist) 29/3/2018 (SEN radio-1116)

"I've seen the great forwards post (John) Coleman: (Doug) Wade, (Peter) McKenna, (Peter) Hudson, (Jason) Dunstall, (Tony) Lockett... This bloke is the closest to Ablett in his ability to just do things that defy the opposition, whatever they do. You can't stop Franklin. It's impossible. I think he's on a level with Ablett. When Franklin plays like he did on Sunday (Franklin in his 271st game against eventual Premiers West Coast had 21 disposals, 9 marks and kicked 8.1), and he's done that dozens of times. You cannot stop him. It's beyond anyone's ability to contain him."

Luke Hodge

(Franklin's former captain at Hawthorn. They played 156 games together and won two premierships) 29/03/2022 (SEN radio-1116)

"He kicked a lot of bags, but when I thought 'hang on, this bloke really could be anything', was when he kicked seven against Adelaide in our first experience in a final... 2007, yes he'd been playing for a couple of years, he'd already kicked a number of goals, but it was just the composure... Bud kicks one from 50 on the boundary with about 30 seconds to go and we win the game by a couple of points and you sit back and go, yes this bloke has got so much ability, but sometimes the occasion can get on top and be bigger than what the player can handle... Not for Bud. He went back, kicked the goal, he's done the double cobra, got us our first finals win and from then he hasn't looked back, has he."

Luke Hodge

29/03/2022 (SEN radio-1116)

"In 2013 we played him on the wing the whole year because we knew we weren't going to have him in 2014 and Jarryd Roughead wins the Coleman...The two biggest games in 2013 for us was the last two finals where we had the Kennett Curse against Geelong. Bud comes into the leadership group meeting and says 'Look, whenever I've played deep I haven't had much success on Tom Lonergan, why don't I push him up the ground and I'll let the other forwards do the work?' So in the big games, he's selfless. And then in the Grand Final he walks in and says the same thing playing on Luke McPharlin... We hear talk about Bud and what he's been able to do kicking 1,000 goals, but he's also had that selfless mindset in big occasions to put the team first and to play up the ground... That's why when he left Hawthorn to go to Sydney, no one cracked it and no one abused him because he was selfless on the two biggest games of that year. We broke the Kennett Curse, we won the Grand Final after falling short the year before... that's why Bud is loved by his teammates."

Sam Mitchell

(Hawthorn Coach from 2022, and who also played 171 games with Franklin, winning two premierships). 18/03/2022, *AFL.com.au*

"Coaches have a ''What if?' meeting normally where it's about 'What if this happens? What if that happens? What changes there?' And I would say half of every coach's meeting ever playing against Lance Franklin has been about 'What if Lance Franklin does this? How will we fix it? And then what if he does that how will we fix that?'... When you have a player who can have so much influence over the opposition's coaches' box, you know you're in pretty elite company."

"When I think back to Lance it's of that growing era of him. When he first walked in he was this young jubilant kid who ran and kicked. He ran as fast as our fastest player. However fast they ran, he ran as fast. He didn't know what he could do. Over time he became more self-aware and started to understand his own talents and really utilise them. It was brilliant watching him grow up and mature and grow into himself as a player first and then as a person later."

Chris Fagan

(former Hawthorn assistant coach, Brisbane Lions Coach from 2017). 18/03/2022 *AFL.com.au*

"When he was a young bloke he was just such a mad trainer. He wanted to be good. He was a great athlete and he's got great skills, but they're not there by accident, he's worked really hard to develop them… His capacity to kick goals for a man of his size, to be able to do it more like a rover at times, he practised that a lot. He's not the great player he is by chance. I think he has an entertainer's mindset. When people go to the footy they go there to watch him… When we trained, he was always one of the last blokes off because he'd be out there doing dribble kicks and kicking them around the corner. All that stuff you'd see in a game, he practised that. It was his playground really, the footy field, and anywhere within 50m of goal."

Jason Dunstall

Buddy 300th game tribute FOX Footy, 23/10/2019

"I will never forget the first final in a number of years that Hawthorn played in 2007, after Alastair Clarkson took over in 2004 and managed to recruit Buddy Franklin… '05 we had a tough year, '06 we improved and '07 we managed to make the finals. Buddy Franklin turned in one of the most amazing individual performances you've ever seen – he tore Adelaide apart. He kicked 7 goals and the last one was the winner under pressure with just seconds to go. I thought 'we have a serious superstar on our hands'."

GARRY LYON

Buddy 300th game tribute *FOX Footy*, 23/10/2019

"Buddy kicking his 100th goal at the then-Telstra Dome, back in 2008... at just 21 years of age, and in only his fourth season, it was the confirmation that we were witnessing the emergence of a footballer with rock star appeal. The crowd invasion after he kicked his 100th, and the scenes of him being escorted off the ground for six minutes while they tried to clear the fans, only added to the hysteria surrounding this young superstar."

ALASTAIR LYNCH

Buddy 300th game tribute *FOX Footy*, 23/10/2019

"Round 13, 2010. Hawks trailed Essendon by a goal in the fourth quarter at the MCG... Bud, already acknowledged as one of the most gifted athletes in the game, took it to another level. Taking the ball 100 metres from goal, at full speed... Three bounces and swinging out towards the boundary, slots one from the tightest possible angle to not only set the Hawks up for another win, but the goal of the year and one of the most iconic goals of all time."

KEVIN BARTLETT

***Marngrook Footy Show*, 30/3/2017**

"I don't know whether we've ever seen a player, six-foot-five in the old, 199cm, be as mobile, be as athletic... He can play fantastic in the midfield – his midfield kicking is just superb, probably even better than when he's in front of goal, but I think that's improved as well... I don't know whether we've seen anyone of his size who can do what he does... Certainly he's the most exciting player in the game – no doubt about that. He's a game changer. Not too many guys can be a game changer, but we saw last week, two of those great goals, 65 metres out, kicking those goals and nearly winning the game for Sydney."

John Longmire
(Sydney Coach) Franklin's 1,000th goal, SEN 2022

"You have to savour those moments... with our players and our staff and Lance's family, we got them all in and we had a chat and spent some time together and the boys weren't in too much of a hurry to have a shower, we sat around and enjoyed each other's company and had a talk about it... It was fantastic to be able to do that... Alastair Clarkson came down with his wife Karen, that was important too because we have to acknowledge that he's obviously played a significant part in Hawthorn's history and a lot of those goals were kicked at Hawthorn, so it's really important to have Alastair there as well."

John Longmire
Buddy Tribute 18/03/2022, AFL.com.au

"Since he's been here (Sydney), there've been so many moments where you look at him and shake your head in amazement at times at what he's able to achieve and what he's able to do on the footy ground for a bloke of that size. He does it so often... When I think of Lance Franklin, I think of a massive competitor. People see the talent, which is there for everyone to see, but when you're in the inner sanctum, you see how much of a competitor he is and how ruthless he is."

CALLUM MILLS

(Sydney co-captain who has played more than 100 games with Franklin). Buddy Tribute 18/03/2022, *AFL.com.au*

"It was a shock, just the size of him. When you're an 18-year-old kid you just can't fathom it. He has this aura about him, but he's also super personable. He shook my hand and said 'hello', even though he didn't know who I was. It's a real testament to his character... He's a big larrikin, a big kid, but he's super friendly and a really good person. All of the boys love him and he'd do anything for anyone."

BAILEY SMITH

(Western Bulldogs player). Buddy Tribute 18/03/2022, *AFL.com.au*

"He's my favourite of all time... I was on the couch at my grandparents' house sweating bullets every time the ball would go near him on the night he kicked his 100th. I've never felt more invested in someone achieving something than that as a little kid... How tall he is and how athletic he is – he is such a threat in the air and on the ground. He's so iconic. He gives me LeBron James vibes how he has performed over a long period of his career and how he can still turn it on."

The last word

It is fitting that the final word on Buddy goes to the man who has kicked more AFL goals than any other. Like Buddy, a giant of the goal square who started at one club and only enhanced his reputation after arriving at the Sydney Swans:

Tony "Plugger" Lockett

"Lance Franklin is a genuine superstar of the modern game, A player that brings spectators to the football... Immense talent and freaky skills see him do the almost impossible on a regular basis. 1,000 goals and All Australian captain. A true champion of the game."